THE NEW BASICS
EDUCATION AND THE FUTURE OF
WORK IN THE TELEMATIC AGE

DAVID THORNBURG

ASSOCIATION FOR SUPERVISION
AND CURRICULUM DEVELOPMENT
Alexandria, Virginia USA

Association for Supervision and Curriculum Development
1703 N. Beauregard St. • Alexandria, VA 22311-1714 USA
Telephone: 1-800-933-2723 or 703-578-9600 • Fax: 703-575-5400
Web site: http://www.ascd.org • E-mail: member@ascd.org

Printed in the United States of America.

April 2002 member book (pcr). ASCD Premium, Comprehensive, and Regular
members periodically receive ASCD books as part of their membership benefits. No. FY02-06.

ASCD Product No. 102005
ASCD member price: $17.95   nonmember price: $21.95

Library of Congress Cataloging-in-Publication Data

Thornburg, David D.
   The new basics : education and the future of work in the telematic age
/ David Thornburg.
      p. cm.
Includes bibliographical references and index.
   ISBN 0-87120-656-0 (alk. paper)
   1. Education—Effect of technological innovations on. 2. Labor
supply—Effect of technological innovations on.   I. Title.
   LB1028.3 .T564 2002
   371.3–dc21
                                                          2001008540

07 06 05 04 03 02 01   10 9 8 7 6 5 4 3 2 1

Dedicated to Luciana, Ana, and Harvey:
the future is yours.

DATE DUE

GAYLORD		PRINTED IN U.S.A.

CONTENTS

ACKNOWLEDGMENTS

Books are collaborative efforts, and this one is no exception. I wish to thank the Federal Government of Brazil for encouraging me to prepare the speech that triggered the writing of this book. Many people I've met over the years have helped me develop and clarify my thinking—George Gilder and other commentators on modern technology among them. To all those whose writings and conversations have helped me understand the challenges of the coming years, I give special thanks. I also want to thank my friends at ASCD for their gentle edits—Joyce McLeod and Ernesto Yermoli deserve special mention.

Most of all, I want to thank my friend, lover, and wife, Norma. She is an emerging-technologies futurist herself, and our conversations together have enriched this book. Her patience during the craziness that marks my writing style is deeply appreciated. I especially want to thank her for the smile in her eyes that greets me when I awaken each morning.

While this book is influenced by many, any errors are mine alone. Any book on the future that makes reference to technology risks appearing dated within a few months of publication. I've tried to stay focused on long-term trends that are less likely to change, even as new technologies appear on a regular basis. For those errors that may emerge, and for the referenced Web sites that seem to vanish without a trace, I convey my apologies in advance and hope that the overarching message of this book remains useful even if the details change a bit.

INTRODUCTION

In October 2000, I had the honor of addressing labor and education leaders from several South American countries in Brasilia, Brazil. My topic was workforce development for the coming years. During the talk, I spent an hour ruminating on ideas about the future of work that had been percolating in my mind for years. In the time since delivering the speech, I have continued to think deeply about this important issue.

Our world is in constant flux; the bases for economic growth are changing around the globe. Developing nations are ascending, established nations are encountering new challenges, and everywhere new technologies are changing the relationships between companies and their customers and suppliers. Yet as these changes transform the workplace and help redefine the very nature of work, schools continue to grapple with curriculum based on the realities of another century, following an educational calendar centuries old. Norm-referenced standardized tests are designed and administered with little or no regard to the future that students will face when they leave school. We continue to talk about the importance of basics, with little discussion as to what basic skills are necessary in today's world. The result is turmoil, with our economy held as a fragile hostage. As I write these words, the United States is rebounding from a dip after the longest sustained growth cycle in its history. As wonderful as this period of growth was, there are already signs that our economy faces incredible challenges in the near future, for which an adequately prepared workforce is essential.

No one knows, in detail, how the coming years will evolve. Instead we gaze at a cloudy crystal ball, grasping only faint outlines and images. This book is about those faint images—the emerging trends that will change the nature of work as the years progress. My main focus is on providing context and rationale for the new "basic" skills that will be required of all workers in all sectors of the emerging economy. While some of these skills are addressed by traditional school curriculum, many of them are not. This book, then, should interest educators and parents who want to instill their students with the habits of mind needed to thrive in the years to come. It should also interest employers as they search for the right mix of talent to keep them on the cutting edge of an ever-changing business landscape.

I'm sure my accounting of basic skills is not complete, and that further "basic" skills will emerge as time goes on. Our dynamic world requires flexibility in everything from the school curriculum to the nature of the workplace itself. This means we must be prepared to add new skills to our list as they become apparent.

The statistics discussed in this book reflect the state of the world in the winter of 2001. By the time this book reaches your hands, some of the numbers I quote will have increased many times over, especially those related to the growth of technology. Though the numbers may change, the ideas they support will, I hope, withstand the test of time. Toward that end, I encourage you to keep abreast of changes in the workplace, the economy, and technology as you chart your own course through the murky waters of the future.

I invite you to come on a journey to your future—the future of work in the "telematic" age.

1

A VISIT TO THE CAVE

Because I write about the educational requirements for the emerging workforce from a perspective outside of school, some of what you will read in this book runs counter to current educational practice. At my presentations on this topic, I have found some who are shocked at the apparent disconnect between the current curriculum and the world at large. It is as if these folks have been living in the cave of Plato's *Republic*, and have now been led outside into a different reality—the one faced by all students as soon as they leave school.

Book VII of Plato's *Republic* (1871/1998) starts with a dialogue between Socrates and Glaucon in which Socrates describes what happens when one's perspective of reality is suddenly changed. As an example, Socrates imagines a cave in which people are chained and forced to look at shadows projected on a wall from behind them. The captives are unable to turn around or to look at anything else but the shadows, and consequently come to think of them as real. Socrates continues:

> And now look again, and see what will naturally follow if the prisoners are released and disabused of their error. At first, when any of them is liberated and compelled suddenly to stand up and turn his neck round and walk and look towards the light, he will suffer sharp pains; the glare will distress him, and he will be

3

unable to see the realities of which in his former state he had
seen the shadows; and then conceive someone saying to him,
that what he saw before was an illusion, but that now, when he
is approaching nearer to being and his eye is turned towards
more real existence, he has a clearer vision, what will be his
reply? And you may further imagine that his instructor is point-
ing to the objects as they pass and requiring him to name them—
will he not be perplexed? Will he not fancy that the shadows
which he formerly saw are truer than the objects which are now
shown to him?

This passage powerfully conveys the confusion we experience when
we find our initial assumptions about a situation to be false. Though
we might after a while come to accept the new reality, we would then
have another problem: how do we go back into the cave and tell the
others that what they are seeing is nothing but shadows on the wall—
that reality is altogether different? As Socrates says:

Would he not be ridiculous? Men would say of him that up he
went and down he came without his eyes; and that it was better
not even to think of ascending; and if any one tried to loose
another and lead him up to the light, let them only catch the
offender, and they would put him to death.

The United States had a steady stream of "education presidents"
over the past four terms, and the public debate on educational reform
is often feverish. Parents, educators, and business leaders all weigh in
on the litany of problems facing our schools and offer countless recommendations for improvement. Some argue that more testing is the
route to better learning; others call for more challenging courses within the existing curriculum. While this concern is well intentioned and
clearly needed, the proposed solutions are often offered only from the
perspective of existing education models. This is the view from inside
the cave, where the very structure of school is accepted without question. We encourage our students to do better in math, science, language, history, and so on, without asking if the curriculum itself is
relevant to the world. We expect students to do better on standardized

tests without asking whether the tests in fact measure anything of value. To those who argue for reform from within the cave, Socrates' words speak volumes: "The truth would be literally nothing but the shadows of the images."

I invite you, in the chapters that follow, to step outside the cave and explore the skills necessary for work in the new century. Getting used to the new light may take effort: the disconnect between current educational practices and the needs of the workaday world may seem too great to bridge. You might find yourself saying, "Yes, but . . ." and defending the status quo even in the face of compelling evidence against it. But a new perspective is worthwhile, because unless we understand how the nature of work is changing, we can scarcely expect to prepare anyone for life outside of school.

Developing this new perspective is difficult. It may take time for you to adjust to some of the ideas presented. In addition, if what you come to see makes sense, you'll have to go back inside the cave and explain the new reality to those who have never seen the light. This venture may be arduous, but we must take the journey together in order to prepare our young people for economic viability in the new century. In the last chapter of the book, I'll discuss the journey back inside the cave to win over converts. But for now let's begin outside the cave, as we explore the future of work in the telematic age.

2

THE DIGITAL TORNADO

A digital tornado of epic proportions is sweeping across the planet at light speed, transforming everything it touches. It has affected work, education, play, and virtually every other aspect of our life by allowing us open access to information (along with the challenge of maintaining personal privacy). It gave us the dot-com boom, and left us dot-bomb ashes in its wake. It gave us the capacity to drive through tollbooths without slowing our cars—and to have the transaction automatically debited from our accounts, without using cash. It gave us the world at our fingertips and made global events seem as near as our own backyards. It made globalization possible for any business, allowing craft economies, such as the lace makers of northeast Brazil, to sell their wares worldwide. It brought about the collapse of hierarchies within large corporations and allowed upstart start-ups to wrest huge markets away from well-entrenched old-line companies caught napping. It has transformed commerce in every arena, from buying a car to shopping for music, and it is bringing educational opportunities to those for whom the college doors are closed.

Unlike wind-based tornadoes, the digital one continues to gather energy long after it first appeared. Starting in the Northern Hemisphere (primarily the United States and Europe), this tornado is now sweeping over the Patanal, across the Sahara, and into the recesses of the smallest towns and villages. What follows is a snapshot of a pivotal aspect of the digital tornado: its effect on the future of work in the coming years. My emphasis here is on the kinds of skills needed to thrive in the modern workplace, no matter which economic sector you work in or what kind of job you have.

Assumptions

Any book like this one is biased. While my perspectives will reveal themselves as we proceed, I think it is fair to state my assumptions right from the start.

Assumption 1: Economics is not a zero-sum game.

One country's economy doesn't need to advance at the expense of another's; the continued economic development of the planet benefits all. There will still be temporary dislocations in the workplace, but primarily when one sector of a country's economy does not transform itself in time to remain competitive in the global market.

Take, for example, the assembly of manufactured goods such as televisions. Many years ago, Zenith manufactured its televisions by hand in the United States. Once this practice became economically untenable, the manufacture of TV sets was automated and moved to other countries where labor is much cheaper. Calls to protect manufacturing jobs, whether through tariffs or other means, soon diverted attention from a larger issue: should we have our workforce do comparatively mindless assembly work when the economy needs every available hand for other kinds of jobs that pay better and make better use of our resources? Unfortunately, people have historically seen the challenge in terms of "unemployment" rather than its true name, "re-employment."

The fact is that the old jobs aren't coming back.

In order for assembly line workers in mature economies to earn a living wage, some consumer goods would have to be priced out of the range of affordability for many people. There are notable exceptions to this rule: microprocessors and automobiles, for example. But most consumer goods, including electronics, are now manufactured in countries where assembly line work is still economically viable.

Instead of bemoaning the loss of jobs, we should expand our workforce development efforts. Unions should craft Educational Maintenance Organizations (EMOs) to support lifelong learning on behalf of their members, so that they can learn the skills needed to secure higher-paying jobs if their old ones become obsolete. Make no mistake about it: the United States and other economically well-developed nations have entered the era of lifelong learning. If you don't continually upgrade your skills in this economy, you will quickly become unemployed, and unemployable.

In the meantime, countries with many low-skilled workers eager for assembly jobs find themselves in the midst of an economic boom. As their economies expand, these countries will generate greater purchasing power for their people, thus benefiting the global economy as a whole. Take a glance at the manufacturing locations listed on gadgets in your house and you'll find the names of countries where high-quality assembly is being done in a globally cost-effective manner.

Does this mean that I support free trade? Yes, probably so. I am astonished at the tariffs some countries apply to imported goods in order to defend their own manufacturing base. In the economy of global access, trade barriers seem arcane at best. When massive shipments of intellectual property, worth billions of dollars, flow effortlessly across borders through satellite signals, the image of a customs agent digging through a tourist's suitcase strikes me as hopelessly out of date.

Assumption 2: Economic growth is driven by open standards and virtuous cycles.

We confront standards every day. When you connect your computer to the Internet, you immediately benefit from standards that specify how packets of data are to be sent, assembled, and displayed, no matter what computers are used or whether the signals are sent through copper wires, glass fibers, or the ethersphere itself. The alphabet soup of TCP/IP, HTML, MP3, etc., represents different standards that are the results of acrimonious debates and compromises. They help make the Internet work, even if some of the choices are suboptimal.

Standards are nothing new. In the days of the early railroads, each company laid its own track according to its own method of spacing. In order to run cars on other company's tracks, the railroads had to agree on a uniform track spacing—based, according to legend, on the wheel spacing of Roman chariots (which in turn was based on the breadth of the rear ends of two horses). But while standards allow diverse groups to develop products that interoperate seamlessly, they can sometimes get in the way of progress.

The problem arises when someone finds a better way to do something, such as compress large image files or play back CD-quality sounds. Even though the new method may be demonstrably better than the existing one, the task of changing the standard often seems Sisyphean in scope. Whether formalized or not, standards support the model of increasing returns: the more people who adopt a standard, the greater the likelihood that even more will adopt it in the future. Such a model can drive competing standards—even superior ones— into oblivion. A classic example of this phenomenon dates back to the early days of the VCR, when Sony's Beta format fought head-to-head with Matsushita's VHS format. Even though Sony had the higher quality technology for playing videos, Matsushita was able to get a larger number of movies published in the VHS format. Shortly thereafter, the Sony format disappeared.

The existence of standards doesn't mean that new ideas can't spring into popular acceptance seemingly out of nowhere. In fact, it happens all the time as a result of "virtuous cycles"—positive feedback loops, often driven by open standards, that help grow the economy. A virtuous cycle occurs when a particular standard becomes more popular than others, and therefore more appealing to new entrants to a market. For example, the rapid growth and domination of the Windows operating system over Macintosh has made it easier for software developers to make money by focusing on the Windows platform. This increase in useful software helps in turn to increase the popularity of

Windows, and thereby drives competing platforms out of the picture. Because positive loops lead to the rise of natural monopolies, new entrants have a hard time cracking the market and profit margins can remain quite high.

An excellent example of a positive feedback loop is Linux, a computer operating system developed and maintained by volunteers worldwide and distributed for free. Unlike traditional shareware that may be buggy or limited in its features, Linux benefits from a positive feedback loop: its creators are also ardent users, and they are therefore relentless in tracking down and eliminating bugs as they appear. The open standard under which Linux operates helps to fuel the positive feedback loop. Since the system is amenable to tinkering, the standard is not set in stone and can evolve indefinitely, thus remaining competitive. In fact, Linux has gone from being a college student's personal project to a key element in corporate strategy for companies like IBM, HP, Compaq, and others. Open standards tend to drive positive loops by assuring that each contributor to a development cycle adds to its value without having to worry about being caught in an economic wasteland, pumping development money into supporting a technology susceptible to obsolescence.

Positive feedback loops and nonlinear behavior of a system as a whole have two seemingly paradoxical properties. First, the slightest nudge can tip them from obscurity to general acceptance almost instantly. Second, once the new behavior locks in place, it is almost impossible to dislodge it (consider that the layout of the standard typewriter keyboard was designed to limit typing speed in order to prevent type bar jams in the 19th century). These two properties are sides of the same chaotic coin that can be flipped whenever a new product category enters the marketplace.

The challenge of standards is that their very goal is to block the acceptance of new ideas. On the plus side, they facilitate interoperability; on the negative side, their existence can stifle the acceptance of innovation. For now at least, I rank standards as a necessary evil.

The reason for this apparent digression from our central topic is that the future of work is shaped by both innovation and standards. The mix is variable, but they both play a role.

Assumption 3: There are grand economic cycles that exist over a period of about 50 years.

This observation was made in the 1940s by the Russian economist Kondratieff (who was imprisoned for such heresy only to die an early death), and recently elaborated upon by Peter Marber (1998) in his book *From Third World to World Class.*

Marber points out that each of the Kondratieff waves was accompanied by driving technologies and had its primary economic impact on different parts of the world (Figure 2.1).

Figure 2.1 KONDRATIEFF WAVES		
Wave Period	**Technologies**	**Primary Growth Areas**
1789–1847	Textiles, Steam Power	Continental Europe
1847–1895	Railroads, Telegraph	United States
1895–1948	Telephone, Electricity	Australia
1948–1995	Cars, Electrical Goods, Aircraft	Japan, South Korea, Taiwan, Singapore
1995–2050	Information Tech., Biotech.	Latin America, China, etc.

In reviewing Figure 2.1, it is important to note that *the economic growth of nations implied by these waves is additive.* In other words, the rise of the United States as a power did not drive the economy of Continental Europe to decline as a result. To use a current example, the information technology revolution has had tremendous impact on the U.S. economy, but because the U.S. economy was already strong, the greatest relative impact will be felt elsewhere. The point of this chart is that nations that were *not* major economic players earlier became, and continue to become, more powerful during their respective Kondratieff waves.

Now that my biases are revealed for all to see, it is time to move ahead and explore the driving economic forces that will shape the future of work.

3

THE DRIVING FORCES OF CHANGE

In exploring the nature of work in the future, we must first understand the main technology driving the current Kondratieff wave: information technology (IT). This chapter provides a brief overview of the tremendous advances in information technology to date.

The digital tornado with which our story began derives its energy from two sources: the collapse of the microcosm and the explosion of the telecosm. These contrasting energy sources are of great interest to numerous authors, notably George Gilder, whose book *Telecosm* (2000) explores the topic in far greater detail than I do here.

The Microcosm

The story of the microcosm is, in part, the story of a silicon integrated circuit called a microprocessor—the electronic heart of everything from the personal computer on your desk to the fuel injection controller in your car. Microprocessors are special integrated circuits, each containing many millions of transistors and capable of performing computational tasks that would have stumped the largest computers a mere three decades ago. Transistors are the most ubiquitous objects of mass production in history: by the time you read this sentence, more than a billion new ones will have been fabricated. Circuits containing these devices are found everywhere from supercomputer systems to toasters.

Anyone who has purchased a computer recently must marvel at the awe-inspiring capacity of these now-commonplace appliances. Computational speeds in excess of a *billion* instructions per second were popular in 2000; yet only a decade before, computers costing four times as much operated at one-thousandth the speed of these workhorses. It is no exaggeration to state that the computational power in a musical greeting card exceeds the combined power of all the computers on the planet prior to 1950. In an *Economist* article titled "Untangling e-conomics" (2000), Pam Woodall reported that a 2000 Ford Taurus contains far more computing power than the multi-million-dollar mainframes used in the Apollo program.

The tremendous increase in complexity of integrated circuits over time is represented with astonishing accuracy by Moore's Law (named after Gordon Moore, cofounder of Intel). In 1965, Moore observed that the complexity of integrated circuits seemed to double every 18 months, while manufacturing costs for a given circuit declined over the same period. Though he never intended that his observation be glorified as "law," it has proven incredibly robust: each new generation of microchip has obediently taken its place along the seemingly inex-orable path of exponential capacity growth. This increase in circuit complexity arises from technological advances that allow, among other things, for more and more transistors to be crammed onto a chip smaller than your thumbnail. We are now at the point where we can build single integrated circuits containing over a billion transistors—a level of complexity unimaginable in the days of discrete circuits made from individual transistors or (gasp!) handmade vacuum tubes.

And yet, someday, we will reach the limit of what we can make on the surface of a pure silicon wafer. The connections will be too nar-row to handle the current, the transistors too close together to oper-ate without interfering with each other, and the generated heat so concentrated it will be hard to remove. At that point Moore's Law will either be retired or, more likely, alternative technologies will emerge to keep us on the path of increased power using new devices. When will the path end? No one knows for sure. But by 2010 or 2020, new computing devices will probably emerge that are even cheaper to produce—and far more powerful—than anything made in the silicon foundries of today. Moore's Law may run its course, but we will continue to meet the demand for greater power and lower cost.

One consequence of Moore's Law is that electronic devices have not only become ubiquitous, but so numerous as to be virtually invisible. FM radios the size of hearing aids can be purchased for a few dollars. Casio manufactures a watch with a built-in digital camera. Sony has a pen-sized device that plays MP3 music files. Cell phones are so commonplace that they will overtake traditional telephones in some countries by 2002 or sooner, and may outnumber televisions worldwide by 2003.

By nature, the microcosm pulls everything toward the center, collapsing transistors and chips until they become irreducible because of quantum limits. At the other extreme is the telecosm—a world of infinite bandwidth that expands everything to the periphery. The telecosm is growing at an even faster rate than the microcosm.

The Telecosm

If the microcosm is the world of computation, the telecosm is the world of communication—and communication, by definition, requires at least two parties. If the microcosmic sphere spins to the sound of Moore's Law, then the telecosm revolves around Metcalfe's Law. Named after Bob Metcalfe, principal inventor of the Ethernet (the technology behind most local area networks), Metcalfe's Law says that the power of a network grows in proportion to the square of the number of nodes (connections). So double the number of connections, and the power increases by four; triple it, and it increases by nine.

The telecosm is the poster child for increasing returns. Imagine it is the early 1970s and a Xerox salesperson pays you a visit to show you a new device called a "telecopier" (today we call it a fax machine). You'd ask what you could do with it, and the salesperson would say that you could send documents to people without using a courier or the post office (there was no FedEx then). Well, that would be fine if you knew other people with telecopiers, but if you didn't, then the only thing this machine would do is suck power out of the wall.

Thanks to Metcalfe's Law, fax machines quickly reached a critical transition point at which they became useful to businesses and homes. Suddenly, fax machines were ubiquitous; we went from asking people "Do you have a fax?" to asking, "What is your fax number?" This same phenomenon happened with telephones long before the telecopier, and years later with the Internet. As with the railroad (itself a communications business), standards played an important role in the sudden transitions of obscure technologies into indispensable communication devices. Whether the technology was telegraphs, telephones, fax machines, or the Internet, Metcalfe's Law took effect only when everyone adopted the same protocols for sharing information. Once this happened, the technologies took off.

We have entered an era of astonishing growth for communication technologies. While the old-line telephone companies are trying to extract every dollar imaginable from the vast copper mines beneath our streets, the photonic future is unfolding literally at light speed. All-optical networks, made of glass rather than copper and operating at several trillions of bits per second, are already a reality. Such networks could transport the content of the entire Library of Congress in about ten seconds. (The current collection, stacked end to end, is about 525 miles long. Assuming five books per foot and 50,000 words per book, you can do the math.)

Optical networks not only carry more information, but they do it at a lower cost than copper-wire holdovers from the golden age of analog telephony. As bandwidth becomes nearly infinite, it becomes, like computing, nearly free. Many have speculated that soon we'll be making unlimited global phone calls for a low monthly flat fee. (Avid Internet users already have this service.)

The challenge of glass is that it is great for the long lines, but awkward for the trip from the curb to the home. Here is where a hybrid approach, probably using wireless systems, can play a critical role. As technology continues to improve, completely wireless systems are sure to emerge that will threaten the hegemony of wire and glass-based systems. End users won't care as long as the connections are cheap, reliable, and fast.

Telematics:
Where the Microcosm and Telecosm Intersect

As mentioned before, the forces of the microcosm pull toward the center, and those of the telecosm expand to the periphery. The tension between these two types of forces is held in place by a combination of technological domains called telematics. Telematics is the place where microcosm meets telecosm, and where each leverages the power of other. Moore's Law multiplies at an even faster rate in bandwidth, compounded by Metcalfe's Law, with the result of ever cascading exponential growth in combined power that drives the digital tornado. While cell phones have made telematic power ubiquitous, the Internet has garnered greater attention than any other telematic resource—and for good reason.

The Internet

The Internet fascinates many observers today simply because of its critical role in the economy of the coming years. From its modest start years ago as a research network for universities and government-sponsored laboratories, the Internet has doubled in size every year; only in 1999 did the growth rate seem to slow a bit. According to Internet watcher Mark Lottor (2001), the number of Internet hosts— each serving from one to thousands of users—went from 56 million in July 1999 to over 93 million a year later.

An accurate count of Internet users is hard to make, but some have estimated that by December 1999 there were 171 million people online worldwide. This number grew to 304 million by the following March, and is projected to exceed one billion by 2006, with 700 million users living outside the United States. The most popular use of the Internet is through the World Wide Web, with a reported size of one billion pages in January 2000 and double that number just six months later. A back-of-the-envelope calculation based on this trend suggests that the number of posted Web pages will exceed the population of earth by 2002.

But it is the use, not the size, of the Web that is most interesting. When I'm asked what the future has in store for us, I always say, "Look at your computer keyboard—it's right there in front of you: Shift Control." As IBM chief Lou Gerstner said, "The rise of powerful networks is about many things, but primarily it is about the transfer of control" (1998). Truer words were never spoken.

Need evidence? Consider this: in 1999, 71 percent of male new car buyers in the United States either researched or bought their cars online, armed with accurate cost information that makes haggling obsolete (NUA Internet Surveys, 2001). And the United States is not alone. In 2000, General Motors introduced a new car in Brazil called the Celta. They decided to sell the car both through traditional dealerships and directly to customers online, at a time when only 8 percent of Brazilians had access to the Internet. So what percentage of sales was made online? Two percent? Eight percent? The actual figures were much higher: 50 percent of all Celta sales came from the Internet! Though the Web has yet to make it into most Brazilian households, its impact is already being felt. A trip to a Brazilian shopping center shows why: in the hallways, along with stands selling cell phones, artwork, and crafts, you are likely to encounter Internet kiosks where people can rent time on a broadband network by the hour. On most days, these services do a brisk business, especially among aficionados of online games and people who want to check their e-mail before going home. In October 2000, the president of Brazil announced a plan to get 30 percent of Brazilians online by 2003. Although this number isn't huge by U.S. standards, consider that Brazil is only recently getting its infrastructure to the point of widely available broadband access. (Computers are also more expensive there than in the United States.) Is it any wonder glass fibers are snaking their way through the Brazilian countryside at a prodigious rate? Control is shifting to the hands of consumers worldwide.

Like many online services, the Celta site allows customers to specify the desired features of a car, which is then built accordingly. In effect, the online Celta customer is also a Celta designer. Likewise, customers of Amazon.com not only purchase books but post reviews as well—making them both readers and critics. This blending of roles is commonplace in the telematic era. The capacity to play multiple roles online makes the Internet far more than an alternative retail channel. Telematics not only lets people do things differently, it also lets them do different things, and this is where its greatest power lies.

As if new relationships with consumers were not enough, telematics has also revolutionized business-to-business transactions. The trend toward mass-customization—in which unique products are built and shipped almost as though from a traditional assembly line—would not be possible without just-in-time inventory, which requires a tight loop connecting manufacturers to their suppliers. Most dynamic companies have moved procurement online and forged tight telematic links with their suppliers, some of whom may even be competitors— leading to the awkward neologism, "coopetition."

Moving beyond Web-based services, we enter the world of such peer-to-peer applications as Groove.net, where users share workspaces on each other's computers without using a central server. An early peer-to-peer system, Napster, captured tremendous attention as a medium for distributing music. The initial attention on Napster focused on copyright infringement, mostly ignoring the fact that the network reached 23 million domains in 16 months—a feat that the Internet required 16 *years* to accomplish.

It all seems very exciting, but has it contributed to the economy? According to the U.S. Census Bureau's *Statistical Abstract of the United States* (2000), information technology contributed one third of the real economic growth in the United States from 1995 to 1999. Since 1993, this sector has added over one million jobs (many of which remain unfilled, but more on that later) to the U.S. workforce (U.S. Census Bureau, 2000).

This tremendous growth is not particular to the United States. If the Kondratieff waves are anything to go by, Latin America, China, and others should truly come into their own this time around. In the short term, this means that the countries in South and North America and South East Asia deserve close attention, with others sure to gather steam soon.

Factors Driving Growth in the IT Sector

Along with the United States and some other parts of the world, Latin America is experiencing tremendous growth in its IT sector (as the comments on Brazil attest). Four basic factors are driving this growth worldwide:

- Cheaper Personal Computers (PCs)
- Demassification
- Infotropism
- Free Internet Service Providers (ISPs)

Let's explore these in turn.

Cheaper PCs

Over the last few years, retail prices for personal computers have dropped dramatically, resulting in more and more home users purchasing PCs. Prior to the mid-1990s, complete computer systems, including a monitor and printer, sold for over $2,000. Today's general-purpose systems retail for less than half that amount, and complete systems can be purchased on sale for $500 or less. Some ISPs, such as Microsoft's MSN, even make it possible for you to get a system for free, as long as you sign a multiyear contract. And the number of people who use their home computers to gain access to the Internet is rising: according to a study by NUA Internet Surveys (2001), 60 percent of the U.S. population had Internet access from home in December 2000, up 15 percent from the same period a year before. This means that over 155 million individuals in the United States had Web access by the end of 2000—and the number continues to grow. More people than ever before find the Internet useful in their lives, and the declining cost of powerful computing systems has made this access more affordable than ever.

Demassification

Another driving force behind IT sector growth is "demassification"—the shift of information resources into nonphysical forms.

19

Consider, for example, the multivolume encyclopedias that once graced many homes. These expensive compendia often took up an entire shelf, and got bigger with each annual update.

When the CD-ROM was invented, that entire shelf could suddenly be replaced by an interactive CD that cost less to make than did a single volume of its print counterpart. At less than 5 percent of the physical mass of a print encyclopedia, CDs are more compact, less expensive to publish, and more reasonably priced. They are also easier to search: someone interested in a particular topic can search for related words no matter where in the encyclopedia they appear—an impossible task with the printed paper version. The next step was to remove the mass from the encyclopedia entirely by posting it on the Web. Online encyclopedias offer all the benefits of the CD-ROMs, in addition to being updated regularly—often daily.

Demassification makes data both less expensive and more useful. This positive feedback loop has driven mass out of diverse informational resources (shopping catalogs, for example) and has functioned as an effective driving force for technology in our homes as well as at work. There is a risk to demassification, however: by relying on access to remote resources, we might eventually run out of bandwidth.

With the Internet continuing to double in size almost yearly, and with an estimated user base of over 400 million whose volume of data traffic doubles every hundred days or so (NUA Internet Surveys, 2001), it is reasonable to wonder when an informational bottleneck will bring the system to its knees. In fact, bandwidth capacity is at present increasing faster than the demand. The key term here is "infotropism," a word coined by George Gilder.

Infotropism

The concept of infotropism is simple: just as plants grow toward the light (phototropism), networks grow toward the data and users (infotropism). Of course, in the case of a network this growth is not natural; it must be planned and effectively executed. Clearly, areas devoid of reasonably priced broadband risk becoming informational wastelands with a limited capacity to thrive in the new economy.

Conversely, communities that bring cheap bandwidth to the masses have a critical element in place that can ensure economic viability in the coming years.

For example, the economy of Pernambuco, a Brazilian state whose capital is the port city of Recife, is expected to grow 20 percent faster than the economy of Brazil as a whole. Recife, at the eastern tip of South America in the northeast of Brazil, was founded by the Dutch in the early 1600s and has always been a significant port. Traced with canals and a river whose docks date back to the 17th century, Recife remains home to a large shipping industry; boats line up for miles off-shore, waiting their turn to enter. Recife is also home to one of the most beautiful beaches in the world, Boa Viagem, whose white sands stretch for five miles and are a magnet for worldwide tourists. Cruise ships frequent the area, and the beach is populated year-round by international visitors. The port and the beach alone are probably enough to support a viable economy for the three million residents of the greater Recife area.

Recife is growing because it is home to a port of another kind: an information portal, providing interconnections and gateways to the world. While Recife has always had a strong connection to information workers (75 percent of the Ph.D.s in the northeast of Brazil live within a 50 km radius of Recife), the high-tech aspect of the city is really starting to take off, aided in part by infotropism.

The same story is unfolding in cities around the world. The availability of broadband brings with it new economic opportunities. In an era where every business is global, high-speed access to the Internet becomes increasingly important, wherever you are.

Consider for a moment the plight of the business traveler who needs Internet access on the road. Not too many years ago, it was common to find hotel rooms without any spare phone jacks to use for checking e-mail. (I used to solve this problem by getting one at a local Radio Shack and installing it myself. I always left the new jack installed, and saw myself as a kind of Johnny Appleseed for wired travelers.) Today, however, the situation is quite different. Virtually every hotel room now has a desk with an electric outlet and phone jack for your computer. Many rooms are even equipped with direct Ethernet broadband access to the Internet for a flat rate of about $10 per day—a bargain for the otherwise bandwidth-impaired.

Airports have always been among the most wired places on earth; after all, air traffic controllers need to have the best access money can buy. But this capacity has only recently started to trickle to the terminals. The infotropic movement is unstoppable, however, and many major U.S. airports now have Internet cubicles or kiosks that can be rented in 10-minute increments, offering—in the slogan of Laptop Lane, one such provider—"Peace, Quiet, and a T-1 Line."

While airline club rooms have yet to yield to the force of infotropism, they at least provide their customers with phone jacks and power outlets so that some tasks can be accomplished between flights, even if at a poky 56k. It won't be long before these clubs wake up and respond to the clear desire for more bandwidth.

Who is providing the world's bandwidth? As mentioned in the previous chapter, telephone companies play a role, but if we just left it to them we might be stuck with slow hookups for decades to come. Everyone, from oil pipeline companies to electric utilities and railroads, seems to be getting into the business of bringing bandwidth to where it is most needed. (Sprint, for example, was created by Southern Pacific railroad initially to bury fibers alongside railroad tracks.) Any business that controls real estate miles long and a few feet wide might find itself courted by those wishing to run glass fibers under their property. These glass fibers are installed in large bundles, with most of the strands left "dark" (unused) to accommodate future demand. As demand increases, the dark strands are illuminated, and the infotropic force continues to spread.

But how can we bring broadband access to homes and workplaces worldwide? This is the so-called "last mile" problem. Most of us live in areas where vast bandwidth lies within walking distance of our front doors, yet we still have trouble bringing this resource into our homes. The problem is that backhoes don't obey Moore's Law: the actual physical wiring of our homes lags behind the increase of backbone bandwidth capacity. For example, when I'm in the United States, I live just a few miles from Motorola's worldwide headquarters. Our Chicago suburb is home to many leaders in the high-tech industry, yet we are lucky to get reliable telephone service. Cable modems and digital subscriber lines (DSL) are unavailable—and no, I don't live on a farm. But our community is sufficiently remote that we lack the local infrastructure needed to wire our homes for broadband. In fact, I have far faster Internet access in Brazil than I do in the United States. This situation, of course, will change, and maybe because we'll bypass glass and copper altogether and go straight to wireless. Infotropism ensures that we'll get the bandwidth we need; if the telephone companies don't provide it, someone else will.

Free ISPs

In her excellent book *The Death of Distance,* Frances Cairncross (1997) notes that the incremental cost of carrying signals on today's networks is fast approaching zero. In the near future, we might not pay for phone calls at all, and pay only a flat monthly fee to our service provider. Once signals are converted to digital form and launched as packets over a network (instead of tying up a dedicated circuit for the duration of the call), a phone conversation halfway across the planet will cost no more than a call to the local store. This instant digital transmission is why ISPs generally charge flat rates for their service: because all their traffic is digital, there is little to be gained by using measured rates.

How much should the monthly fee be? Some ISPs have eliminated their connection fees altogether, thus providing an even greater impetus to the tremendous growth in Internet access worldwide. ISPs offering free services generate revenues from Web-based services, such as flower delivery. Other free ISPs bombard their users with advertisements. The feeling among these providers is that by growing their user base, they expand the potential customer base for their other products and help build brand loyalty.

Inexpensive PCs, demassification, infotropism, and free ISPs have resulted in a rapid increase in new Internet users. Within a few short years, the Internet and the World Wide Web have gone from mere curiosities to foundations of commerce. We may not know the details behind the jobs of the future, but we can be fairly certain that meaningful access to the Internet will play a role in virtually all of them.

4

WORK IN THE TELEMATIC AGE

Some futurists like to think in terms of ages or epochs: long periods in history characterized by a unifying theme, the most common of which is economic development. Alvin Toffler popularized the trend of dividing history into economic units with his writings on the Agricultural Age, the Industrial Age, and the Information Age. George Gilder, on the other hand, based his model of ages on abundance. According to Gilder, whatever a society perceives as abundant tends to become a prodigiously expendable resource—and in so doing, representative of its age.

Abundant Resources Through History

Time

Gilder points out that to the agrarians, for whom life revolved around the seasonal cycles of planting and harvest, time itself was an abundant resource (2000). This meant that people could spend a long time on a single project. For example, the great cathedrals built during the Agricultural Age took hundreds of years to construct; the stones at the top of these structures were cut and placed there by the grandchildren of the masons who started the project. Tasks of a scope exceeding a single lifetime stand in stark contrast to the fast-paced work of today. While some see Frederick Taylor's time-motion studies (1911/1998) as the driving force behind this change in standpoint, he was merely refining and quantifying a shift from the agrarian perspective to a more modern view, in which time was seen as a factor to be measured and controlled (rather than as the natural flow of nature).

It is impossible to stand at the base of the Cathedral at Chartres, or any other from the late Middle Ages, and not be amazed at the diligence required to build it. It is also hard to imagine a project of this magnitude being undertaken today. Long-range planning these days focuses on the next quarter; a five-year plan is considered ambitious indeed. Many of us lead hurried lives, rushing from task to task, trying (often unsuccessfully) to fit downtime into our jam-packed schedules. Books and tapes promise to teach a new language in thirty days, how to get your point across in thirty seconds, and so on.

Technology played an integral role in the evolution from the agrarian view of time to our present-day perspective. The invention of the mechanical clock gave us an accurate way to measure time, rather than relying on roosters to wake us in the morning. The railroads created a need for time zones, so that schedules could provide accurate arrival and departure times for long-distance train travel. The concept of "efficiency" accelerated our passion for spending time wisely. The net effect of these changes is that we now are almost at the opposite end of the spectrum, time-wise, than were our agrarian ancestors. Though we've paid the price in increasingly hurried lives for our focus on productivity, we have clearly gained much as well.

Coal and Iron

Because factories were powered by water at the beginning of the Industrial Age, they had to be built near rivers. With the advent of steam-powered factories, however, location was no longer an issue. By the Victorian era, coal and iron had become abundant resources, and factories sprung up wherever they could be found. The plains of the United States were soon paved with iron rails so that iron horses could carry the seeds of economic expansion out west. The black coal smoke billowing from locomotives became emblematic of progress, and it's

25

no wonder why: the abundance of coal and iron allowed for the efficient inward expansion of nations. This view drove the economy to new heights, and brought us to the dawn of our current era.

Electricity

Electricity took a long time to catch on. Competing standards—specifically, direct current (Thomas Edison's plan) versus alternating current (George Westinghouse's plan)—impaired interoperability for many years, but by the time we settled on alternating current, electricity was already in use. Initially, large, single motors driving belts on a linear assembly line replaced steam engines in factories. It took time for people to realize that each tool could have its own motor, thus allowing for a more efficient reconfiguration of the workplace. In fact, the dispersal of motors throughout a factory made less efficient use of electricity while at the same time improving the efficiency of the factory, by allowing for the placement of various independently motorized machines on the factory floor. This shift toward decentralized motors was facilitated by the accompanying view that electricity just flowed out of wall sockets for free (a perspective still held by our children when they forget to turn the lights off as they leave a room).

In the 20th century, electricity became an abundant resource that we could use to operate domestic robots, thus eliminating live-in servants. These robots—in the form of washing machines, dryers, dishwashers, and microwave ovens—transformed the home life in profound ways that touched every aspect of the house, from entertainment consoles to electric blankets. The idea that electricity could be used with abandon changed the lives of everyone—including housewives, who were now sufficiently freed from domestic burdens to be able to earn income on their own.

Transistors

By the 1990s, transistors had become abundant enough to waste. These microscopic electronic devices form the foundational elements of integrated circuits, and are found in a wide variety of products, from barbecue forks with built-in thermometers to wristwatches; as I mentioned before, they are the most ubiquitous products of mass production ever fabricated.

Transistors allow us to embed mechanized "intelligence" in all kinds of products. Once embedded, integrated circuits help operate your electronic wristwatch, focus your camera, control your toaster, and keep your house at the right temperature—in short, they silently perform important tasks without announcing their presence. In my presentations, I sometimes ask people to guess how many computers they have in their homes. Initially, they will choose a low number like one or two. But once I mention the seven or so computers in a modern automobile, not to mention the video games and other microprocessor-controlled devices found in many homes, the number quickly rises. We probably don't even know how many microprocessors we have in our homes, any more than we know for sure how many electric motors we have. In fact, the first clue we have that these devices exist comes when they break down—a phenomenon more likely to happen with motors than with embedded microprocessors.

But are all transistor-based devices really necessary? After all, we were able to toast bread quite adequately when toasters contained simple thermal-mechanical release mechanisms instead of microprocessors. Our homes were perfectly comfortable with mechanical thermostats, and our parents were able to drive long distances in cars that had no computers in them at all. So why did we decide it was appropriate to use transistors in devices that never needed them before?

First of all, transistorized appliances are cheaper to make than their purely mechanical counterparts. By standardizing on a controller circuit, an appliance manufacturer can produce a full line of devices that use the same microchip, with different programming for different functionality among various models. The high production volume of these devices helps keep their cost down to pennies, and the lack of moving parts means they last longer, thus reducing service costs and eliminating the need for an inventory of spare parts.

Secondly, powerful microcircuits can provide appliances with features that were inconceivable with purely mechanical devices. Self-focusing cameras, for instance, need transistors in order to work properly, and have in recent years evolved to provide spot focus on whatever object the eye focuses on through the viewfinder; additional circuits counterbalance the jitter of camera motion. Other new features, many of which were unheard of in the days before transistorized cameras, have improved the focus and contrast of photographs. The photographer is thus free to spend more time on other issues, such as visual layout. As with electricity, a perceived abundance of a particular resource produced an overall improvement in efficiency and productivity.

The impact of transistors on our lives is far from over. The next wave of capabilities will come when our appliances start communicating with each other. For example, Electrolux makes a refrigerator with a built-in bar code scanner. Whenever food is removed from the fridge, it is scanned into the refrigerator's memory by a bar code. When the supply of certain foods is low, the refrigerator can automatically place an order with an online grocer using a built-in connection to an Internet service provider; the online grocer then delivers the food to your door. In principle, you could check the status of milk at home from your handheld computer while at the grocery store by e-mailing your fridge to have it check its own contents. Similarly, a computer in your stove could check the electronic pantry and recommend a dinner menu that you could check remotely from work.

These examples may seem a bit farfetched, but they are logical extensions of current practice, driven by the expendability of transistors. Already we can see the consequences of this phenomenon on the workforce: automotive repair shop workers, for example, clearly need to know about the computers in the cars they service. These high-tech skills are now required for workers in many fields that were only recently purely mechanical. These days, wrenches and software go hand in hand.

Bandwidth: The New Abundance

The wide availability of transistors pales in comparison to the emerging abundance of bandwidth. While it is true that many people still log onto the Internet via slow dial-up phone lines, in the near future broadband services will be virtually everywhere. As a result, we will soon be engaging in richer electronic interactions than ever before.

For someone with dial-up access, the adage "a picture is worth a thousand words" literally holds only if the images are compressed to about 40 kb; any larger and they become bandwidth hogs. This is why some people criticized the first really popular Web browser, Mosaic: it allowed access to images as well as to linked hypertext. But when dial-up modem speeds increased to a rate of about 50 thousand bits per second, graphic images—along with other bandwidth hogs, such as sound files and small movies— became more and more common.

Many people have made the quantum leap from dial-up to cable modems or digital subscriber lines (DSL), which have data transfer speeds of a million bits per second or faster. The popularity of such tools as Napster and Gnutella—which facilitate the downloading of large music files—proves that demand will meet the supply, no matter how quickly the data is transferred.

The bandwidth revolution fills a deep need by allowing us to send information in far richer formats than plain text. The abstraction of unformatted text at one extreme gives way to the concreteness of deeply textured media, the richness of which is almost tangible, and more personalized electronic communication than ever before. As bandwidth increases, the ability to download CD-quality sound, or movie images as rich as theater projections, is just around the corner. But even this won't be enough. We will always push for greater quality and deeper richness in communication, and for our electronic media to bring us as close to a face-to-face discussion as possible.

This urge for greater realism is not the only reason behind the expendability of bandwidth. Increasingly, more and more communication will take place between appliances and computers without human mediation. Automobiles will automatically connect to remote databases to check if the internal programs on the onboard computers need to be updated. Because the silicon in most cars is already worth more than the iron, our autos and other appliances will almost certainly reach the point at which they initiate diagnostic and repair dialogues on their own while we sleep.

The implications of broadband communication technology for the workforce are clear. First, many people will need to acquire technical skills to maintain and develop networks. Second, all of us will need to become effective communicators: in order to ensure maximum impact for our ideas, we need to become effective communicators adept at various media.

The Knowledge-Value Era

While Gilder's model of abundance offers fascinating insights, others have also made significant contributions to a historical perspective on work. One of the more articulate thinkers in this arena is the Japanese consultant Taichi Sakaiya, whose 1991 book *The Knowledge-Value Revolution* provides a powerful context for thoughts on the changing nature of labor.

Published before the Internet exploded into its present form, Sakaiya's book contrasts three distinct periods in history: the era of the guilds (the Middle Ages), the Industrial Age, and the present day, which he calls the Knowledge-Value Era. Sakaiya characterizes the current period as one in which product value is based more on knowledge content than on material. A designer scarf made from a dollar's worth of silk sells for many times that price because of its knowledge value— that is, the value of the design itself. We are clearly living in a world where the price of many goods, especially high-end ones, is determined by aesthetic rather than material considerations. The most extreme example, of course, is computer software that has no physical component; yes, software is often frozen onto CD-ROMs or other physical media, but the medium serves only as a carrier, not as an integral part of the product itself. Furthermore, when software is sold online and downloaded directly from the developer's computer to the customer's, no physical medium changes hands at all; the transfer is purely informational, and its value is completely determined by the knowledge that went into its creation.

Sakaiya points out that this was not always the case. In the time of the guilds, workers owned their own tools and practiced for years

30

alongside masters to learn their craft. But the skills these workers learned were usually measured against a rubric of quality that changed slowly if at all, providing little room for personal expression. Stonemasons working on a cathedral learned to cut stones in a certain way and to a certain size; because each stone had to fit perfectly with its neighbor, variations were neither appreciated nor permitted. Even so, mastery lay in the hands of the workers, who owned both the tools and their hard-won skills.

During the Industrial Age, capitalists owned the tools. Furthermore, labor was divided into decontextualized chunks, so that workers became largely interchangeable units. Rather than laboring as apprentices for years, workers could be trained in the requisite skills within a few hours. The growth of low-skill labor in factories was a byproduct of Eli Whitney's assembly line for mass production, in which each worker repeats a different task over and over again. As raw materials make their way down the line, they become finished goods without any one worker having done more than his one specific chore.

Due to the interchangeability of labor in an assembly line, Industrial Age workers were detached from a sense of pride in a completed project. Consequently, managers needed other incentives to maintain product quality. Many took to the "scientific management" view of Frederick Taylor (1911/1998), which posited workers as mere elements of the production process who could be manipulated like farm animals. (Taylor referred to workers as "oxen.") The characteristics valued in Industrial Age workers were punctuality, comfort with piecework, and blind obedience to authority—all attributes reflected by the schools of the period, with their focus on strict time schedules, compartmentalized information, and rigidly applied rules and tests.

As automation decreased the need for low-skill labor on the assembly lines, the Industrial Age gave way to our current Knowledge-Value Era, in which workers *are* the means of production. Today, tools are often secondary to the creative processes of workers; the intellect and application of ideas are what drive the current economy. The tools of the modern worker are largely informational and commonplace, and can even be found in most western homes. The real value workers bring to their jobs lies in their knowledge and creativity. As Berkeley professor Ikujiro Nonaka once told me, "The dynamics of knowledge are the most competitive resource of the firm." It isn't just knowledge, but the *dynamics* of knowledge—its changing nature—that is valuable in the modern era. Increasingly, this change in knowledge comes from workers at all levels.

From a company standpoint, the challenge is clear: if the real value lies in the intellect of workers, then their departure can cause a venture to fail. In the Knowledge-Value Era, power has shifted into the hands of employees. Work is no longer interchangeable, and people can no longer be treated like cogs in an industrial machine.

The New Basic Work Skills

The opportunities for workers in the Knowledge-Value Era are as clear to them as the challenges are to management. With the requisite skills, these workers can auction their work to the highest bidder and move from one company to another, leveraging expertise and salary at the same time. In the Industrial Age, people often spent entire careers working for one company; today, highly skilled workers hop from contract to contract on a job-by-job basis. Even full-time employees often switch jobs every year or so, virtually impervious to the ups and downs of any particular employer. During the recent rash of dot-bombs, companies coupled their layoff announcements with demands for talented workers, yet our educational system remains largely unchanged since the Industrial Age; the times they are a-changin', but our schools remain outdated. Given the transformations of the Knowledge-Value Era, today's workers need to learn completely different skills than did their Industrial Age forebears.

Another thinker who has written about this topic is Robert Reich, whose book *The Work of Nations* (1992) was published just before his appointment as Secretary of Labor. According to Reich, the quality jobs of the future will belong to "symbolic analysts"—people who solve, identify, and broker problems by manipulating images. As Reich says:

> [Symbolic analysts] simplify reality into abstract images that can
> be rearranged, juggled, experimented with, communicated to
> other specialists, and then, eventually, transformed back into

reality. The manipulations are done with analytical tools, sharpened by experience. The tools may be mathematical algorithms, legal arguments, financial gimmicks, scientific principles, psychological insights about how to persuade or amuse, systems of induction or deduction, or any other set of techniques for doing conceptual puzzles.

The rise of the symbolic analyst is the direct result of a shift from global competition to global alliances, which have made it increasingly hard to identify the nationalities of major companies. The recent rise of truly global corporations has not only opened new markets for goods and services, but has allowed jobs to migrate to countries with more efficient labor regulations. Certain U.S. assembly jobs, for example, have moved to countries where labor costs are lower than in the United States. If these jobs were not allowed to migrate, assembly-line employment would still decline in the United States due to the rise of automated manufacturing. On the other hand, jobs that require the skills of a symbolic analyst are on the upswing, and pay great dividends: symbolic analysts can ply their craft worldwide and be remunerated handsomely for their efforts.

Whether we refer to modern laborers as symbolic analysts or knowledge-value workers, they all have several characteristics in common. According to Reich, the basic work skills required by the new class of workers are *abstraction, system thinking, experimentation,* and *collaboration.*

Abstraction, or the ability to discover patterns and meanings, is the core of symbolic analysis. The daily chaos of data that surrounds us requires us to employ abstraction in order to make sense of our world. This skill stands in conflict with the traditional schooling of my youth, with its focus on memorization of isolated facts.

System thinking follows logically from abstraction: it is the ability to think of most problems in the context of a complete system with interrelated elements. This capacity to think in terms of the "big picture" can be developed, and is of increasing interest to both businesses and schools.

Because we cannot accurately predict the behavior of complex systems, experimentation—the ability to try something, note the results, and make modifications until a desired result is obtained—is tremendously important. This skill also requires creativity and openness to serendipity: "Let's try this and see what happens" can often lead to whole new opportunities and discoveries. While Edison, Bell, and other inventors clearly benefited from experimentation, the modern-day director of marketing goes through much the same process as well.

Collaboration is important for two crucial reasons. First, many of the challenges facing us today cut across a wide range of disciplines, which can often only be bridged through teamwork. Second, by interacting with others, we can often discover new approaches to problems that would have stumped the lone wolf forever.

While I explore the skills of the knowledge-value worker in greater depth elsewhere in this book, I would like to identify a few key characteristics here. In addition to having the skills identified by Reich, the knowledge-value worker is likely to be:

- A contractor, not a long-term employee

- Comfortable with ambiguity

- A lifelong learner

- Highly mobile

- Highly entrepreneurial and creative

Let's examine these characteristics one by one.

Contract Work

Because they *are* the means of production, knowledge-value workers are not bound to company equipment. In fact, more and more people are working effectively from home, using equipment they have purchased themselves. Their loyalty, therefore, is to their craft and to those who honor their skills and invest in their continued development. Once a job becomes routine, knowledge-value workers become restless and look for new horizons, either with other full-time employers, or, increasingly, as part-time consultants.

The trend toward highly mobile part-time employment benefits many corporations, too: in an era of fierce competition and swift market expansion, a large and stable workforce can be more of a liability than an asset. MIT's Laubacher and Malone explore the impact of a mobile knowledge-value workforce in their paper, *Retreat of the Firm and the Rise of Guilds* (2001). The authors discuss the effect of newly dynamic work relationships on services that once were provided exclusively by corporations. Companies traditionally provide insurance, pensions, and professional development resources to their long-term employees. But as long-term workers give way to shorter-term knowledge-value personnel, responsibility for these services falls to outside organizations—if not to the employees themselves. Laubacher and Malone suggest that we will see the return of guilds as stable homes for services that meet the long-term insurance and professional development needs of today's dynamic workers.

The authors point out that as of 2001, over 25 percent of all U.S. workers worked part time, as either independent contractors or temporary workers. In high-tech regions, the number climbs even higher: only one in three Californians, for example, holds a traditional full-time on-site job.

The MIT study notes a continuing shift away from the implicit lifetime employment contracts of generations past and toward freelance work based on month- or even daylong contracts. We are seeing the emergence of "spot markets" for expertise measured in hours or minutes, such as in the case of house calls from a family doctor. This approach to labor is now showing up in many other sectors of the workplace, too, from writers to tax lawyers, venture capitalists to graphic designers. Where internal corporate procedures ruled the day a generation or so ago, the dynamics of the World Wide Web seem to have the upper hand today, as evidenced by expert spot markets served by Guru.com or HotDispatch.com.

Laubacher and Malone captured the essence of today's dynamic worker:

> Making a career today no longer means progressing upward within an established hierarchy. Rather, it now involves progressing through a series of assignments that provide continual opportunities to learn. In many situations this represents a return to a craft mentality, where progress is not measured by position, but by growing mastery.

And so there is a new relationship between employees and employers that will continue to evolve in the coming years. Unfortunately, the antiquated accounting practices at many companies treat employees as expenses, not as assets. (For example, an engineer with a salary of $100,000 with a million-dollar idea is treated as a $100,000 expense, not as a million-dollar asset.) Many corporations acknowledge that their most important assets go home at night, but their appreciation can't be measured on the bottom line of a bank statement: while intellectual property is definitely a "hard asset," its specific value is hard to ascertain. This situation may change as companies grow to realize that their informational assets can be traded on the open market, which allows for the quantitative valuations of ideas.

Yet2.com is a patent and license exchange that allows companies to shop for innovations made available by other companies. The entry fee for joining the site ranges from $4,000 to $50,000 per year, and Yet2.com gets 10 percent of any completed transactions. The average technology posted on the exchange is worth about $5 million in research and development. As Yet2.com Vice President Conrad Langenhagen told me, "Companies have this enormous need to understand what they have within their own walls. At Siemens they say, 'If only Siemens knew what Siemens knows, we'd be a great company.'"

Arthur Andersen, the world's largest accounting firm, took a novel approach to learning about the talents of its employees by creating an internal knowledge management project. The idea behind the project was to tap into the tacit knowledge of in-house experts and spread that wisdom throughout the firm. This tactic has resulted in the company's Global Best Practices knowledge base (http://www.globalbest-practices.com), which breaks company business down to 13 elemental practices, with details on how best to implement them. Although the service was initially created for in-house use, it is now available to outside clients for an annual fee that ranges from $10,000 to $150,000.

Comfort with Ambiguity

Comfort with ambiguity follows naturally from the changing nature of the work contract. If you don't know for whom you will be working next month, you are even less likely to know what you'll be doing when a contract comes your way. Couple this uncertainty with the rapidity of knowledge-base change in virtually all professions, and it's no wonder that those who are uncomfortable with ambiguity tend to be highly stressed.

For a futurist, comfort with ambiguity is a survival skill. The rapidity of change, along with "wild cards"—important discoveries that seemingly come out of nowhere—makes forecasting virtually impossible. Some constants appear to hold up for a long time—Moore's law, for example. But as with any such principle, Moore's law carries a hidden assumption: namely, that silicon planar technology will dominate microelectronics well into the future. This may seem like a safe assumption, but you can be sure that there are research groups at Intel and Motorola asking the crucial questions: "What if we're wrong?" "What will be next?" These researchers thrive on ambiguity, and their efforts may well save their companies from extinction when the next wave of technology hits.

How will computers be made in the future? Will we start making plastic transistors that can be silk-screened onto circuit boards? Will we construct computers on printing presses, with different "inks" containing the necessary electrical properties for a complete circuit? If so, does this mean that the powerful PC on our desk today could be manufactured for about a dime? And what about the corner pharmacy? Imagine if doctors could formulate prescriptions from their own offices by "printing" medications onto edible paper tabs with a special ink-jet printer. These suppositions are not flights of fancy, but serious ideas that are being explored in research labs today.

Ambiguity does not diminish the importance of specific skills and areas of knowledge. For example, there is an entire field of study devoted to the analysis of wild cards and their impact on the world: it's called "history." Unfortunately, many of us remember history as a required course full of names, dates, places, and battles, rather than as the story of people making decisions with imperfect information. If there is one subject fundamental to survival in our rapidly changing world, history is it, but not as it is often taught; I remember all too clearly history teachers who felt it their duty to pump as much information into our heads as possible so that we could regurgitate it on a test. Instead, we need to see history as *the story of how things come to be as they are*.

History reveals trends that sometimes replay themselves: Mark Twain is reputed to have said that while history may not repeat itself, it sure rhymes a lot. He was right, and the rhymes of history provide comfort in the face of ambiguity. I think of history not as a circle that repeats, but as a fractal spiral from whose eddies spring the wild cards that lead us to uncharted realms of economic and social development.

The study of art can also help us deal with ambiguity. In art, creative tension exists between the medium involved and the types of expression it facilitates. At the same time, art offers us the freedom to explore new realms within an existing structure. Personally, I experience this freedom through music. As a blues guitarist, I work with well-established patterns; for example, I can say to my band, "Let's do a 12-bar blues in E" and immediately start playing. The overall structure of the piece has been communicated, yet the details of the melody are totally unspecified. I may have a particular solo in mind, but then find that something the bass player does makes me think along different lines. The lead can migrate smoothly to other instruments as we all get into the groove of a piece we have never heard before and will never play again. Sometimes it works and sometimes it doesn't, which is itself an important lesson: not every new idea is a good one. Though often nerve-wracking, improvisational music is a great way to develop a greater understanding of this concept. It doesn't matter if we're practicing in my living room or at a concert in front of 600 people—we still take risks, because when everything clicks the result is tremendous!

The discipline of improvisational art is great training for life, and, in my view, should be an essential part of the curriculum. When you improvise you are fully "present," living fully in the moment; you are guided—but not held captive—by the past, and you treat the future as emergent, with only the barest of outlines in place to lead the way. Perhaps it is the emergent nature of music that led Arthur Schopenhauer to call it the only art form that evokes nostalgia for the future.

An appropriate patron for improvisation is Janus, whose two faces look in opposite directions—one forward, and the other back in time.

If the face looking back represents history, and artistic creation signifies the present, then the face looking forward is symbolic of the next characteristic on my list: lifelong learning.

Lifelong Learning

The phrase "lifelong learning" has become so commonplace today that we rarely think about its real significance. For example, some people nod with approval at the idea while continuing to talk about a K–12 system—as though such a system were not, at its core, antithetical to lifelong learning. The perpetual development of new industries has created a stark reality for students, in that many of the jobs of the future haven't been invented yet. We have scarcely begun to think about what educational institutions would be like if they truly supported lifelong learning. Traditional colleges and universities celebrate the dismissal of cash-paying customers with every graduation, rather than embracing them as customers (rather than mere donors) for life. In fact, the only formal educational institutions that seem to grasp the true nature of lifelong learning are community colleges, which are often looked down upon by their more prestigious four-year counterparts. Consequently, most students graduating from traditional colleges today are left to meet their future learning needs on their own.

Two driving forces make lifelong learning an essential characteristic of successful people: the short shelf life of much existing information, and the exponential rate at which new information develops.

The rapid pace of technological development contributes to the swift obsolescence of much that we know and requires us to update our knowledge on a continuous basis. For example, every time we install a new version of a word processor on our computers, we have to spend some time learning new features and commands. Some people try to avoid this challenge by using old versions of software for as long as possible. This approach works to a point, but someday someone is going to send you a file created with a new program that your old version will not be able to open, and you'll be dragged kicking and screaming to upgrade out of necessity. Sooner or later, half of what we know about certain tasks will be obsolete, and we'll have to rush to catch up.

Short-term knowledge is clearly an inappropriate focal point for traditional education. Every so often, parents tell me that they want their child's school to teach mastery of Microsoft Windows in the classroom. While technological fluency is critical, the standardization of a particular operating system based on the idea that it will still be dominant years from now is unrealistic. While the Windows and Macintosh operating systems continue to evolve in dynamic ways, Linux and other UNIX-based operating systems are increasingly popular. I honestly have no idea what operating system will be dominant ten years from now, which is precisely why the capacity to learn an entirely new system as quickly as possible is so important.

Every few months it seems we come across some scientific discovery that changes our preconceptions about life, or even of the universe itself. In the summer of 2001, the mapping of the human genome was one such event; by the time you read these words, another topic will have transformed our beliefs yet again. Lifelong learning is the only insurance policy against being blindsided by the short shelf life of information.

As I've already mentioned, the exponential growth of knowledge is a great reason to make lifelong learning an essential characteristic of today's workers. While estimates vary, some people suggest that the total amount of information in the world doubles every two years. Let's assume that this is true. Now I want you to do an experiment. Imagine a one-centimeter strip of paper as representative of all the information in a child's world as he or she enters kindergarten. Our entire school system, from kindergarten through 12th grade, is based on this body of knowledge. When the child enters 2nd grade, the total amount of information in the world will have doubled, and our strip of paper will have grown to two centimeters in length. By the start of 4th grade, the strip will be four centimeters long. By 6th grade, the strip will be eight centimeters in length—all the way up to 12th grade, at which point the strip of paper will measure 64 centimeters (Figure 4.1).

Look at what has happened: the paper strip representing the amount of information available to the child has grown from one centimeter to well over half a meter in length by the senior year of high school. If nothing else, this activity shows that our schools should not

Figure 4.1
RELATIVE RATE OF DATA ACQUISITION FOR K–12 STUDENTS

Grade	Relative Amount of Information
Kindergarten	1
2	2
4	4
6	8
8	16
10	32
12	64

be in the information delivery business—that task is untenable in this era of rapid knowledge growth. Until we transform our schools into places for lifelong learning, we should concentrate on developing the *capacity* for lifelong learning among students. Among other things, we must ensure that the desire to learn is never extinguished. Many children enter school as avid learners, but by 3rd grade begin to see learning as drudgery, and start dreaming of a time when they won't have to learn anything ever again.

What would happen if schools worked hard to keep the love of learning alive in students and teachers alike? What kinds of activities would take place in such a school? What would assessments look like? Until we engage in a serious dialogue about these issues, schools will continue to operate as they always have.

How does the successful worker of today keep abreast of new developments when most of our existing educational institutions have not yet seriously addressed the needs of the lifelong learner? Most have taken matters into their own hands, using the Web as a powerful ally. Myriad newsgroups exist online, covering a wide range of topics, and the Internet is full of specialized resource sites for any subject. In the Knowledge-Value Era, a wealth of information is only a mouse click away.

By integrating online tools with more traditional educational resources (e.g., a community college course), the opportunities for lifelong learners are limitless. In fact, the challenge is not in finding enough to learn, but in budgeting enough time to keep abreast of your field (with occasional trips to other areas for serendipitous connections).

How much time should you set aside for learning on a regular basis? One day a week? More? Less? The answer depends in part on the rate of change in your profession. My cardiologist probably spends 25 percent of his time learning new things—knowledge that I am very glad he has. At the opposite extreme, I probably spend at least 60 percent of my time learning new things. As an emerging-technologies futurist, I have to keep my eyes on many developments, and because I lack the time to do it all myself, I often pay others to keep their eyes open on my behalf. In fact, I spend far more time learning now than I ever did when I was in school.

As Ray Kroc, founder of McDonald's, once put it, "When you're green, you grow. When you're ripe, you rot." Lifelong learning keeps you green and growing.

Mobility

Whether hopping from job to job or traveling long distances for a single company, workers are becoming increasingly mobile. Due to the nature of short-term contracts, modern workers often flit from city to city for different clients. Many attend professional conferences in far-flung places; others relocate completely, in search of a better quality of life.

At first blush, increased mobility seems to counter the trend toward more telecommuting from home. Not too long ago, I thought that videoconferencing would permanently diminish business travel. While this may still eventually happen, business travel seems to be on the upswing these days; after all, videoconferencing is a poor substitute for meeting in person, where you can make new friends through casual interaction in the hallways. If the conference has an exhibit hall, the chances for serendipitous meetings are even greater. At present, videoconferencing is best suited to a limited range of applications; in my own case, I find it useful for short client briefings with people I've previously met face to face.

At the same time, technology has produced new opportunities that flip the videoconferencing paradigm on its head: some workers travel so much, they keep multiple homes in different areas near their clients. So where is the "home" office, and how do you maintain a semblance of order when you're always on the road?

The Internet lets us stay at home while traveling anywhere in the world through cyberspace. But it can also function as a virtual home office: you can use the Web to check e-mail, pay bills, balance bank accounts, and do anything else that you would ordinarily do at the office. Because I always check my e-mail right after checking into a hotel on the road, people know they can reach me wherever I happen to be, just about anywhere in the world.

But mobility has its risks as well. As today's highly skilled migrant workers move around the planet, they can lose a sense of connection to "home." A few generations ago, most people lived their entire lives only a few kilometers from where they were born, which helped promote stability, strong family relationships, and a deep sense of community. In a world of increased migration, on the other hand, family ties can often be strained. Community in our new world is based on common values and interests, not on accidents of birth. It is important for highly mobile workers to pick home bases at which they can spend significant amounts of time, and to limit business travel so that roots can be established in at least one geographic community. For contractors, this means turning down some jobs in order to spend time at home. While income may consequently slow down in the short term, a sense of place also provides the kind of personal balance needed to think clearly—which, in the long term, increases value to clients. In my own life, I split my residence between two countries. I have good friends in both places, and spend enough time at both homes to nurture the local relationships. Mobile workers must understand the nature and role of communities, and should use this awareness to decide how much travel makes sense for them.

In addition to moving from place to place, today's workers move from industry to industry. Switching career paths is increasingly common, and many choose to strike out on their own as entrepreneurs. An inter-career lifestyle requires workers to be generalists, and to avoid overspecializing so much that they cannot adapt to new kinds of work. They must also be quick learners, able to see opportunities in different careers and bring fresh insights to new jobs; ideas that may not have worked in one career may take on a new life in another. In some cases, a successful venture in one area allows people to "cash out" and move into new fields—as is often the case with entrepreneurs.

Entrepreneurship and Creativity

Some people are at their most comfortable within the confines of a large corporation. They like being able to focus on a single main job, knowing that someone else has created a safe environment for them. Insurance, retirement benefits, and salary increases are all handled by the human resources department, according to a schedule that predicts the rate of advancement for employees based on their performance. Those who work in this environment are happy to move along a predefined 30-year career path toward retirement, a gold watch, and a modest pension. This model of the workplace was dominant in the United States for years and provided a steady source of labor in a variety of fields, from secretarial work to corporate administration; these days, however, the 30-year employee with a gold watch is an anachronism. Companies are increasingly engaging in massive layoffs under the guise of "right-sizing," and employees who expected the company always to take care of them have become disillusioned and angry.

Downsized employees are finding themselves ill equipped to thrive in the new workplace, but there have always been a few daring souls willing to leave the comfort of established enterprises to start their own companies. Others often scoffed at these trailblazers, and their incomes were so unpredictable that they had to develop new measures of success, such as quality of life or the freedom to live out lifelong dreams; this breed of person is the entrepreneur, setting out on new adventures with no more than an inaccurate map of the potential terrain in hand. Some of them have succeeded beyond their wildest dreams, which has led to the misconception that people start their own companies strictly to make a lot of money. While this may be true for some, I think the common denominator for most entrepreneurs is a sense of pride in building a working enterprise out of an idea. Some are so enthralled with this aspect that they become serial entrepreneurs and spend the rest of their lives launching venture after venture, using the proceeds of successes to finance new endeavors.

Take for example Jim Clark, founder of Silicon Graphics Inc., who probably could have retired quite comfortably when he left that company in 1994. Instead, he teamed up with Marc Andreessen from the University of Illinois that same year and cofounded Netscape. After selling Netscape, Clark could once again have easily retired; instead he started Healtheon/WebMD, an Internet health company, in 1996. Since then, he has gone on to found MyCFO.com and Shutterfly.com, and is probably dreaming of ventures to come.

In my own life, I've seen a true serial entrepreneur in action: my grandfather, Devoe Thornburg. I remember visiting him as a child in Winchester, Indiana, where he had a small real-estate office. As he grew older, his doctor advised him to think about retiring. Since he loved the water and fishing, he and my grandmother moved to a trailer park in Ft. Myers, Florida.

From his "retirement" base in Florida, my grandfather started a fishing charter, a lawn-mowing service, and an old-time hardware store, launching each new venture as soon as the previous one became successful. My grandfather was the textbook definition of a serial entrepreneur. He never went to college, but knew what he wanted to do, and he did it with skill and joy. Though he never became rich, that was never my grandfather's motivation. Through his own example, he taught his son and grandson an important lesson: though entrepreneurs may go through hard times, deep inside they know that, sooner or later, success will emerge.

From what I've described, it may seem that you need to be born with the entrepreneurial spirit; you either have it or you don't. I don't hold that opinion. I believe that each of us can develop the ability to take control of our careers, and that our educational institutions can help with that process. Certain after-school programs, such as Junior

Achievement and 4-H, address entrepreneurial characteristics, but there is even more we can do. For one thing, we need to teach our students that the cradle-to-grave security of the old company model is just a faint memory for most people. Survival depends on acquiring the capacity to create ventures from scratch, and on taking charge of our own lives and successes.

Successful entrepreneurs have several attributes. First, they need to be very creative—to see opportunities where others see nothing. Second, they need to know how to communicate their ideas to others effectively, spreading their visions like viruses in order to attract support and build markets for new projects. Third, budding entrepreneurs need to be self-starters; no one is going to check to see if they're coming in late to their own offices, or if they're completing necessary paperwork on time. In addition to these skills, the entrepreneur needs to adopt the knowledge-value characteristics described in this chapter—especially the abilities to handle ambiguity and be a lifelong learner.

Are those who lack the characteristics described in this chapter doomed to a pitiful existence in the coming years? No, of course not. But those who are comfortable with ambiguity and mobility and are lifelong learners and creative entrepreneurs will have amazing opportunities ahead!

5

A CLOUD ON THE HORIZON

In November 2000, my wife and I went to the movies in Santa Clara, California. As we waited for the film to start, we were drawn into a slide show of movie trivia questions and advertisements projected onscreen. The ads were fascinating: in the span of a few minutes, we counted no less than 17 that offered local employment to highly skilled workers. The companies placing the ads ranged from pre-IPO startups to Fortune 500 giants; in all cases, they made it clear that they were looking for highly skilled IT workers, and that qualified applicants would be richly rewarded. The ads didn't mention salary—high pay was a given—but focused instead on other benefits, such as athletic club memberships, gourmet meals, onsite massage facilities, and laundry and dry-cleaning services. These employers were practically begging for qualified applicants—an impression further reinforced by billboards along Route 101 leading to San Francisco, on which one company after another enjoined highly skilled workers to help them create the future.

My wife and I soon realized that, if you had the requisite skills and could fog a mirror with your breath, there was a job for you in Silicon Valley. And this phenomenon was not just restricted to California—it extends to IT work nationwide.

The Critical Shortage: Skilled IT Workers

Companies today are in a feeding frenzy for high-tech workers. As discussed in the previous chapter, our economy is based in part on an abundance of critical resources; currently, bandwidth and transistors. But IT workers are also a critical resource these days, and their scarcity could lead to a major economic downturn in the near future.

Following the end of the dot-com boom and layoffs among even the larger IT employers in early 2001, it may seem as though the bloom is off the high-tech rose. Nothing could be further from the truth! The overall size of the IT workforce is large and growing, and even if the growth rate slows for awhile, there will still be a large number of available positions for which there are few if any qualified applicants. For example, on March 8, 2001, Intel announced that it would lay off 5,000 workers. The next day, Cisco announced it was cutting 16 percent of its workforce—about 8,000 workers overall. And on the following Monday, the tech-heavy NASDAQ stock market dipped below 2000 for the first time since 1998, as a response to the bad news from Cisco and others. Yet on the same day that NASDAQ hit the skids, the job search Web site FlipDog.com had listings for 26,973 IT jobs in California alone. The number of available IT jobs in the United States on that day was 108,612—and this is from a single site.

The Abundance: IT Jobs

Even as some companies hit hard times, others are thriving—and ones that are floundering now might one day rise again. History has shown that companies can endure periods of trouble and still bounce back quite strongly. It wasn't too long ago, for example, that Apple Computer was considered dead as a company. But in 1997, when founder Steve Jobs returned to the helm after an extended absence, the company began to recover; in the end, it needed to rehire more people than it had laid off when times were tough. And the well-established companies like Apple aren't the only ones hiring; additional high-tech ventures that need highly skilled workers pop up every day. Unless we start providing workers with IT training early on, the gap between the number of available jobs and the number of qualified applicants will continue to grow.

According to the Information Technology Association of America (ITAA, 2001), the United States currently has an IT workforce of about 10 million—three times more workers than the auto industry and ten times more than the steel industry. Unfortunately, there are more jobs available than workers to fill them. ITAA projected a shortfall of more than 843,000 workers for early 2001—that's one in 12 U.S. jobs. Unless a change comes soon, the U.S. Department of Commerce projects that the number of unfilled jobs will grow to 1.3 million by 2006.

Now to get a sense of what this means, imagine what the Industrial Revolution would have been like had we run out of iron ore. It would have fizzled! Yet that scenario is precisely analogous to our current situation: we have a demand that far outstrips our supply. Fortunately, high-tech workers (unlike iron ore) can always be created.

Job Categories in the IT Sector

The ITAA study points out that, contrary to popular opinion, a plurality of IT workers dwells in the South. So much for the California mystique! The greatest demand for new IT jobs—35 percent—is in the Midwest; California has 28 percent of the total demand. For the most part these jobs are being offered by relatively small companies, which are eating up the supply as quickly as it's produced. In 2001, for instance, companies with fewer than 100 employees are projected to hire a million IT workers—70 percent of the total IT demand. These employers are looking for people who can hit the floor running, so a good knowledge base in the job area is essential. This does not, however, mean that companies value only technical skills: lifelong learning, flexibility, communication, and problem-solving skills rank highly as well.

There are eight major job categories in the IT sector.

Database Development and Administration. These are the data analyzers, knowledge architects, systems analysts, and others who create databases for end users. These workers need to be able to approach problems creatively and provide access to data while maintaining system security.

Digital Media. These are the artists, animators, audio/visual engineers, multimedia authors, and others who create riveting presentations to effectively relay messages in various media, including Web sites, training videos, and computer simulations. Because digital media technologies are continually evolving, workers must always stay on top of the latest innovations in their fields. In the end, it is through the creative visions of these workers that their employers achieve customer recognition.

Network Design and Administration. These are the information system administrators, network analysts, and support specialists who make sure computers are running smoothly; they are also the network "gods" that add new users to their companies' systems and manage the connections between local networks and the Internet. These workers need to be able to quickly identify, document, and solve problems, and to possess a deep understanding of technology.

Programming/Software Engineering. These are the computer engineers, software design engineers, software testers, and architects who design and create software. In addition to writing code, these workers are also involved in design and problem solving; they need to be familiar with several programming languages, as well as to know how to document their work.

Systems Analysis and Integration. This category covers a wide range of jobs, including application integrators, data warehouse designers, information systems planners, and systems architects. The primary task of these workers is to ensure the smooth functioning of complex information technologies as they interact with each other and their users. In other words, they facilitate interoperability. Workers in this career path need to be able to perform high-level design and system integration functions.

Technical Support. The customer service representatives, help desk technicians, product support engineers, and support personnel who make up this category are a vital contact point between high-tech companies and their customers. Because they work directly with customers, these workers often gain valuable insights about issues that need to be considered in future product releases.

Technical Writing. These are the writers, documentation specialists, technical editors, and desktop publishers who clarify technical information through their manuals, Web sites, and training materials. These workers also need to understand the elements of good graphic design, and must also be creative, have excellent communication skills, and possess the ability to explain complex topics in understandable language.

Web Development and Administration. The Web architects and designers in this category are the Webmasters who determine the look and feel of a company's site. In addition to the technical skills associated with Web site authoring, such as HTML coding and Flash animation, these workers must be good designers: a proficient Webmaster is one-half engineer and one-half artist.

As you can see from these categories, there are a wide variety of jobs in the IT sector with diverse skill requirements, ranging from the highly technical to the highly artistic. The effective blend of these skills drives up the worker's value to a company. Clearly, a high school education alone is probably inadequate training for workers in any of the categories. An additional two to four years or more of education is virtually a requirement, as is ongoing education throughout one's professional career.

So why the shortage of skilled workers? After all, these jobs look pretty exciting. They have lots of room for individual expression and continued skill development, and they pay very well. For example, in 2000, when the average U.S. salary was $30,000, the average salary for IT workers was $53,000—with some job categories paying much more than that! Whatever reasons there are for a shortage of qualified workers, poor salaries are not a factor. Neither is boredom: these are highly creative and dynamic jobs, nothing like the extremely repetitive work of assembly lines. Most IT workers have no idea exactly what they will be working on a month from now; their world is one of endless new projects and challenges.

Immigrant Labor and On-the-Job Training

A lot of attention has been paid to the many immigrants working in U.S. IT jobs. The H-1B visa program, for example, allows foreign workers to stay in the United States for a period of up to six years if they have the necessary skills to secure a high-tech job. This program has its critics and supporters. On the one hand, there are those who suggest that there is no worker shortage, and that the visa program is just a ploy to take high-paying jobs away from able U.S. workers and give them to get cheap foreign laborers. On the other hand, critics complain that the cap on H-1B visas is set artificially low and that the annual quota gets filled up before the year is half over, leaving potential employers in a severe bind.

Often left out of the debate over visas is the fact that the IT worker shortage is not specific to the United States. For example, Nokia, a Finnish company, hires more engineers each year than graduate from all the colleges in Finland. Obviously, the company has no choice but to look outside its country for qualified workers. Still, there are alternatives to the direct importation of foreign labor, such as hiring overseas telecommuters. This way, the employer avoids having to deal with the Immigration and Naturalization Service (INS)—a painful process for anyone. Anyone who thinks that U.S. employers hire foreign workers because it is an easy solution to the domestic employment gap has obviously never dealt with the INS. Telecommuting can also be cost effective, because it allows the employer to pay wages commensurate with those of the worker's home country.

A lot of companies these days see job training as a solution to the worker shortage. I live a few miles from Motorola's global headquarters, which is also home to Motorola University. This school in Schaumburg, Illinois, offers a wide range of courses that would be the envy of many traditional universities, and gets a steady stream of students from Motorola facilities worldwide seeking career development. In fact, the corporate university has become commonplace among large companies. Hewlett-Packard, for instance, has a long tradition of offering courses for employees—in some cases even using staff from Stanford University, which is located next to the company's main campus. Sun Microsystems even offers some course materials to the public for free. But smaller enterprises—those that are currently hiring the most IT workers—don't have the resources to create their own in-house universities, and therefore need a more creative approach. These companies often form alliances with local community colleges, which can even offer courses tailored specifically to the company's needs. As online educational opportunities increase, so too does the capacity for companies of all sizes to provide their employees with ongoing educational opportunities.

While immigrant labor and on-the-job training may help resolve some of the challenges facing companies today, we still need to address the pressing issue of workers entering the job market for the first time who lack the necessary skills to secure high-paying IT employment. These jobs are all technical, which means that an in-depth education in math and science is essential. Indeed, because advances in science and engineering increasingly shape our world, math and science instruction is just as important for those *not* pursuing high-tech jobs. Unfortunately, many of today's graduates lack a solid education in either field.

Igniting the Pedagogy of Passion

A report by the National Commission on Mathematics and Science Teaching for the 21st Century (2000), chaired by U.S. Senator John Glenn, lists a variety of reasons for improving math and science education. Among these are the demands of the changing economy; the links between math, science, and national security; and at a fundamental level, the need for informed citizens in a democracy. The report also points out that in 2000, 85 percent of U.S. jobs were classified as "skilled"—compared to 1950, when 80 percent were classified as "unskilled." According to Richard Judy at the Hudson Institute (as quoted in the Glenn study), 61 percent of all new jobs require skills that only 20 percent of the workforce possesses.

In its report, the Glenn commission offers specific recommendations for improvements in education. The commission suggests, for example, that high school math and science teachers should hold degrees in their chosen fields. After all, if teachers of math and science are not mathematicians or scientists themselves, how can they possibly succeed at inquiry-based instruction, in which students work on real math problems or conduct scientific experiments? Teachers whose backgrounds are in fields other than the ones they teach tend to rely on the more traditional instructivist, or "teaching and telling," method of teaching, which may help students learn the vocabulary of a topic, but essentially digs no deeper than providing responses to multiple-choice tests.

The report also notes that we need to entice more teachers into the classroom. These days, the demand for fully qualified math and science teachers far outstrips supply; according to the commission, 48 percent of middle schools and 61 percent of high schools reported difficulty finding qualified science teachers. The problem is even worse in urban areas, where 95 percent of the high schools queried reported an immediate need for qualified math and science teachers.

The main reason behind the dearth of qualified teachers is not hard to fathom: it is a dedicated person indeed who forgoes the substantially higher pay of an industrial career in order to become a teacher. Many educators also feel that the school system does not recognize and honor their expertise—leading to low morale and a high turnover rate.

The Glenn commission argues that high-quality teaching is essential for students if they are to attain the levels of achievement in math and science necessary for high-tech career paths. While the commission's goals are laudable and their recommendations sound, there is one additional reason for having mathematicians and scientists teach math and science: their passion for the subjects.

I have met many students who understand the basic concepts of math and science, and might even have latent skills in them, but who have no interest in exploring the subjects outside of school. These students have spent years learning about math and science without learning *why* mathematicians and scientists exist. Why have some people chosen to devote their careers to the exploration of problem areas for which solutions may not be found in their lifetime? This kind of understanding can't be found in high school textbooks, and it isn't measured on our tests. Yet without it, we miss an opportunity to ignite the flame of passion that students need if we want to entice them into these fields.

I've seen firsthand the importance of understanding as a key element in developing a passionate interest for a topic. My youngest daughter, Luciana, received passing grades in math and science, but never showed much interest in the topic. One day Luciana saw a picture on my laptop of an orbit trap for a chaotic function I was exploring. The picture was quite attractive, and Luciana's artistic bent was piqued by what she saw. When she asked what it was, I told her it was mathematics. She didn't believe me. To her, math was all numbers and calculations. Although these attributes are obviously elemental to mathematical understanding, Luciana's limited conception of the topic was as absurd as thinking that mammals consist only of mice and wolverines—accurate as far as it went, but highly incomplete. She was startled to find that I woke up every morning and did math "on purpose"—that I actually had fun with the subject. In short, she had spent a decade learning about math and science, but had spent zero years learning why there were mathematicians and scientists.

And it's not just math and science—teachers in all subjects face the challenge of turning their students on to what they teach. It was only well into high school that I had the good fortune of having a history teacher who helped me understand why there are historians; I can still remember the fire in his eyes as he explained the research he had done on his doctoral thesis on the Panama Canal. My fear is that teachers themselves often don't understand the passion some of their colleagues feel for their subjects, and are thus poorly equipped to ignite this passion in others. Until we honor the pedagogy of passion as highly as we do the pedagogies of learning, we will never get enough highly skilled workers for the workforce of the future.

6

NEW SKILLS FOR A NEW ERA

Thus far we've explored the ways in which technological progress affects employment, as well as the negative consequences of an unprepared workforce to our economy. Now it is time to examine in detail the specific core skills necessary for most of today's workers, and to identify the ones that schools should embrace as part of the curriculum.

A logical starting point for our journey is the Business Roundtable (http://www.brtable.org), an organization of senior business executives devoted to improving education. The organization began focusing on education in 1989, as a result of a presidential challenge from George H. Bush to business leaders to help improve U.S. schools. Business leaders were quick to respond, because even over a decade ago it had become apparent that while the percentage of high-skill jobs was rising, the number of highly skilled job applicants was not. As a result, the Business Roundtable started working to increase expectations for all students and helped shift the debate from "inputs," such as seat time and cost per pupil, to "outputs," such as how well students have mastered subjects.

While the energy and devotion of the Business Roundtable to education is laudable, the group erroneously assumed that the existing curriculum and testing process is appropriate for today's world, and devoted its efforts to improving student performance within the existing system—instead of enticing people out of Plato's cave for a dose of reality.

In order to ascertain what skills should be taught in school, we need to begin by examing the world outside the cave. Once we identify the skills students will need to thrive in the workplace of today and tomorrow, we can move on to explore how to modify the curriculum and measure student mastery. To assume that the existing curriculum is fine as it is reminds me of an old definition of insanity: if insanity means doing the same thing over and over again and expecting different results, then it is sheer lunacy to assume that the existing curriculum is fine as it is.

In the past, identifying the skills needed for the workplace was hard work; when asked to name a few of them, senior executives would speak in terms so broad as to be virtually meaningless. Fortunately, the Internet has made our task much easier. An associate of mine, Bob Kenyon, pointed out to me that there are many Web sites available for those seeking employment. Sites such as Monster.com and FlipDog.com contain thousands of job descriptions from companies all over the country, and most of them list the skills required. Research on fundamental skills that used to take months can now be done in hours; and because job listings change daily, skill lists can be updated on a regular basis. Job descriptions can even be isolated by locale, so that regional needs can be quickly identified. Most importantly, because the skills are identified in connection with actual job openings, there is no question about their validity; if a skill is listed, it is required, period.

The New Basics

Using Web-based resources, I examined 500 job descriptions, posted in the Spring and Summer of 2001, that mentioned specific skills. I restricted my study to full-time, non-apprentice positions from a wide range of industries—including restaurant and hotel management, heavy equipment manufacturing, retail, and pharmaceutical companies—in a variety of locales, and constructed a table of the six most wanted workforce skills.

Before exploring this table in depth, let's be clear on one point: the list is not based on opinion, hunches, forecasts, or guesses, but on research that you yourself are invited to replicate using the Web. Although your percentages may differ by a few points, I am confident that the net results will be the same. Though we may disagree on how best to ensure that students learn these skills, there is no point in arguing whether they are in fact required—they are.

Technological fluency is required in over 80 percent of the jobs I looked at; the skill was a virtual given for most of the position descriptions I studied, and I didn't focus on high-tech jobs. Simply stated, technological fluency is the capacity to use computers and the Internet as naturally as you would books, pens, or paper.

Three-quarters of the jobs I studied counted communications skills as a prerequisite. This skill transcends the capacity to write and speak well: many of the job descriptions mentioned proficiency with computer-supported presentation tools (such as PowerPoint) as a necessary qualification. You can have the best ideas in the world, but unless you can express them concisely and clearly they will never be implemented.

Teamwork was mentioned explicitly in 36 percent of the job descriptions, but was implied in many more. With very few exceptions, the lone-wolf worker is an anomaly these days; collaboration—along with leadership, the fourth most wanted skill—is required at virtually every level of a modern company.

The remaining two high-scoring skills, problem solving and creativity, were also implied in many more advertisements than the raw numbers indicate. Numerous job descriptions described successful applicants as ones with a high tolerance for ambiguity, who could solve problems, think "outside the box," demonstrate strong analytical skills, and learn new procedures, tools, and ideas quickly.

It is heartening to see that a list similar to mine was adopted by the CEO Forum (http://www.ceoforum.org) in their *School Technology and Readiness Report* (2001), using information from the NCRELsponsored enGauge project on 21st century skills (Lemke, 2001). According the the enGauge project, the core skills necessary for the present-day worker are:

1. Digital-Age Literacy

- Basic scientific, mathematical, and technological literacies
- Visual and information literacies
- Cultural literacy and global awareness

2. Inventive Thinking

- Adaptability/ability to manage complexity
- Curiosity, creativity, and risk taking
- Higher-order thinking and sound reasoning

3. Effective Communication

- Teaming, collaboration, and interpersonal skills
- Personal and social responsibility
- Interactive communication skills

4. High Productivity

- Ability to prioritize, plan, and manage for results
- Effective use of real-world tools
- Ability to create relevant, high-quality products

In addition to the skills I found and those listed by enGauge, such characteristics as appreciation and understanding of cultural diversity, pride and excellence, and something called "high tech, high touch" were recurring themes in the Web-based job descriptions I studied.

High Touch

The phrase "high tech, high touch" first appeared in John Naisbitt's 1982 book, *Megatrends*, and formed the basis of *High Tech, High Touch* (1999) by Naisbitt and others. According to Naisbitt and his colleagues, "high tech, high touch" can be defined as follows:

> It is embracing technology that preserves our humanness and rejecting technology that intrudes upon it. It is recognizing that technology is an integral part of the evolution of culture, the creative product of our imaginations, our dreams and aspirations— and that the desire to create new technologies is fundamentally instinctive. But it is also recognizing that art, story, play, religion, nature, and time are equal partners in the evolution of technology because they nourish the soul and fulfill its yearnings. It is expressing what it means to be human and employing technology fruitfully in that expression.

In today's hurried workplace, workers often become so caught up in tasks that they lose sight of the big picture. This hurts their capacity to perform effectively at work, as well as hurting them personally; stress often builds up to the point where personal relationships and health suffer. The problem-solving and creativity skills increasingly required by today's employers take a severe hit when workers lose sight of a balanced life.

Technologies designed to liberate people from mundane tasks and to provide improved customer service often have the exact opposite effect when blindly applied. When companies feel pressured to improve productivity, they sometimes reduce the number of people assigned to a task, assuming that improved information technology can allow the same work to be done by fewer people. The consequences of trading people for technology are immediately apparent to anyone who has called an 800 help line for a major institution. Instead of talking with a human being, the caller is usually guided through a maze of prerecorded messages. Unfortunately, the customer whose need is most urgent rarely has an appropriate option from which to choose, and is therefore relegated to the netherworld of "hold hell" until a fellow human being can take the call. When a real-life person finally does get on the phone, the company representative must inevitably deal with the caller's wrath over time wasted on hold in the name of improved efficiency. When we allow our technologies to be used in ways that diminish the human spirit, we do our society a disservice. The world of high tech can be wonderful, but it can also enslave us. For this reason, it is essential that those who work in the pressure cooker of today's workplace find a balance between high-tech skills and the "high touch" skills of life. People whose lives are their work rarely make good workers. They may clock extraordinary hours, but their health, creativity, and problem-solving and communication skills suffer. It is therefore as important as ever for people to find activities outside the workplace that nourish the human spirit—activities that stretch the mind, body, and creativity, drawing us into a place where we are free to experience and learn from childlike wonder.

Those who argue that their time is too precious to spend writing poetry or kneading bread dough by hand miss the point. First, our health depends on far more than earning a living. Second, many business leaders have strong interests outside of work—interests that keep their creative juices alive and make them more effective at work. Hewlett-Packard hired medieval historian Carly Fiorina to turn the company around, Compaq entrusted its future to rock guitarist Mike Capellas, and Classroom Connect was cofounded by R&B piano player Rem Jackson. This list could extend longer than a trip on one of Malcolm Forbes' motorcycles, because people with a balanced life are more effective workers than those who focus exclusively on their jobs.

In my own case, as an emerging-technologies futurist, I feel most fulfilled exploring the countryside with my wife or playing the blues on guitar. In fact, if I had to choose between computers or guitars, I'd give up my computers in a heartbeat. The fact is that my guitar playing has made me a better presenter by providing me with insights on topics related to work. My wife, Norma, is also an emerging-technologies futurist. One of her creative outlets is sewing and embroidery, and there is no question that the problem-solving skills she develops with her craft help her with work as well.

Such real-world evidence of the influence of "high touch" skills should be of great comfort to educators who fear the loss of their arts programs in the face of a return to "basics" (as if there were something more basic than art!). But we must still pay very close attention to the foundational skills identified by the Glenn commission and others.

Short-life vs. Long-life Skills

Technological Fluency

The existing curriculum fills the day to overflowing, and if new skills are being added to a full plate, something needs to first be removed to make room. Fortunately, I think there is a litmus test that can help determine whether a particular skill should be taught in school or acquired elsewhere, such as through on-the-job training. We need to start by drawing a distinction between two kinds of skills: those with a short shelf life, and those that will remain relevant for a long time. Skills relating to specific operating systems or to specific software titles are "short-life" skills, because they cease to be relevant as soon as a new version of software replaces the old one.

The heated debate a few years ago as to whether schools should continue to use the Macintosh operating system when they were going to graduate into a "Windows world" missed the point. Operating systems are "short-life" programs, whereas the proper focus for education should be on long-life skills. While schools still have to decide on a platform to use in class, this decision must be based on factors other than which system is most popular among corporations at a given time. The key is to define the kinds of tasks that students will be responsible for, and to choose the software and operating system that best perform these tasks. For some tasks, Windows is the clear choice, for others it's Macintosh, and for still others it could be Linux or some other flavor of UNIX.

If the choice of operating system is not central to my definition of technological fluency, then what about specific software titles? For example, shouldn't every student become conversant in PowerPoint? Not necessarily: PowerPoint is only one of several programs that can be used to create presentations. Other programs are less expensive and even better, if not as popular. Furthermore, PowerPoint will, hopefully, evolve over time, and the version that students learn today might be far different from the version they encounter when entering the workforce. The same argument applies to the choice of word processors, databases, spreadsheets, web browsers, and all the other tools that are used in classrooms. All of these specific tools will have migrated to new versions with new features and new command structures by the time students enter the workforce.

So, if all computers programs are short-life tools, what is left for schools to offer students? The answer is simply this: we teach children to use whatever software we happen to have available at a given time, but with a focus on the bigger picture, rather than on the minutia of mastering some obscure feature exclusive to that particular program. In other words, when we teach students to use word processors, our focus should be on the writing process and on presentation—issues of font selection, margin size, and the use of headings, for example. Although students will learn how to do these tasks using a set of commands specific to the word processing program used, they will know that the skills themselves will apply to any system they may confront in the future.

Students need to know how to use technology effectively to create documents, locate information, collaborate with remote groups, perform calculations, and make dynamic presentations. At minimum, they should understand how to use the following tools:

- the Web
- peer-to-peer workgroup software
- word processor
- spreadsheet
- graphing software
- database
- drawing software
- paint/photo software
- sound and music creation/editing software
- animation/movie editing software
- presentation tool (including multimedia authoring)

There are two main reasons why this list is a starting point in our quest for technological fluency. First, students will likely use the skills needed to master these tools for the duration of their eventual careers. And second, these tools can be used effectively to explore other academic topics, making them essential not only for students, but for teachers as well.

If you will accept for the moment my list of tools that students should learn, let's turn our attention to the concept of "fluency." Fluency transcends merely *knowing* how to do something; it means doing things almost automatically, without being conscious of every little step, like driving a car or riding a bicycle. Want to create a document? Just boot up the word processor and start typing. This level of comfort with software is exactly what employers are looking for. They expect their employees to know which tools are best for which tasks, how to use them effectively, and how to deal with new versions of software on their own. The goal, after all, is the project, not the tools.

The only way I know to achieve fluency in any field is to use the tools so much that they become second nature. In order to do so, the tools must be available at anytime, wherever they are needed; if students have to trek to the lab just to use a word processor, it is hard to imagine them ever becoming fluent in its use. Some may argue that schools don't need to focus on technological fluency when most students have Internet access at home, because the students will simply pick up the necessary skills on their own. While it may well be that home-based computers help familiarize students with the use of hardware, there is no guarantee that students can develop effective strategies for analytical work when left to their own devices. There is a world of difference between knowing how to send e-mail and knowing how to compose a message that effectively conveys your ideas, and a teenager is not likely to pick up this latter skill during late-night sojourns online.

Statistics on student use of the Internet speak volumes to the challenge we face. According to *Teenage Life Online* (2001), a report for the Pew Internet and American Life Project (www.pewinternet.org), 73 percent of U.S. youth between the ages of 12 and 17 use the Internet. While 94 percent of these teens report using the Web for research on school projects, and 71 percent report that the Internet was a major source of information for their most recent school project, only 5 percent said that they learned how to use the Internet in school; 40 percent were self-taught, and the remainder learned from parents, friends, or siblings.

Before we celebrating this as evidence of self-directed learning, keep in mind that comfort with the Internet does not necessarily imply knowing how to use the tool effectively. As the Pew study documents, teens rely on "gut sense" or "I know it when I see it" rules to determine the accuracy of online information. Clearly, they need help learning how to evaluate information properly; unfortunately, even though almost all schools in the United States are now wired to the Internet, we have failed to mandate the instruction of foundational information literacy skills to students at an early age.

Communication Skills

The core of educational practice lies in teaching students to express themselves well; educators have been teaching their charges to speak and write properly for as long as schools have existed. The challenge today is in incorporating other expressive modalities, such as graphics and animation, into the curriculum. We have already established that knowing the details of a specific presentation tool is a short-life skill. Schools should instead concentrate on long-life skills, such as effective presentation design; for instance, students should understand that documents designed to be read in print should be conceived differently than presentations projected on a large screen. (Lynell Burmark explores this topic in greater depth in her 2002 book *Visual Literacy*.)

Unfortunately, very few educators have received instruction in these skills themselves. Furthermore, most educators were taught by college professors, a group that is not generally well versed in effective presentation design. If you doubt this, attend any education conference yourself and look closely at the presentations given by university faculty. You'll find presentations for which the visual aids are simply transparencies of the handouts; the projected material is scarcely legible to the presenter, let alone the audience. Ever since college and university faculty adopted computers as presentation tools, they've by and large been content to use canned presentation templates for pure-text presentations riddled with more bullets than the St. Valentine's Day Massacre.

Overly busy presentations, too, can be just as bad as bare-bones ones. Left to their own devices, students will often go out of their way to create presentations that make rich use of images, sounds, and animations. On the surface, this willingness to embrace other expressive media is wonderful; too often, however, these projects are little more than eye candy, obscuring any actual content. Unsuspecting teachers may get so caught up in the beautiful slide transitions and scrolling visual effects that they might not notice the lack of substance.

I speak from experience. Fortunately, I also found a way to help students develop effective presentations without stifling their creativity. I simply informed my students that their presentations would receive two grades: one for the presentation design and one for the content. Their final grade would be the product of these two grades, rather than the sum; in other words, there were two ways to get a zero (poor content or poor presentation), but only one way to get a high grade (high levels of both). Students quickly learned the importance of having both excellent content and a well-designed presentation. Of course, this rubric only made sense if I actually taught the students effective presentation design, and I saw this as one of my duties as their instructor. After all, my focus was on the development of lifelong skills that could be used forever, regardless of changes in technology.

The Function of School

The skills that were most often mentioned in the online job descriptions I studied were all long-life skills that I believe should be taught in our classrooms. Every one of the skills on my list can be developed within the context of any given subject. It is never too early to start developing the skills necessary for the workplace of tomorrow.

When I share my observations with educators, they sometimes argue that it is *not* the function of schools to prepare students for the world of work. While I agree that education has other purposes, such as creating an educated populace necessary for a democracy, I am startled to hear the view that our educational system should not be used for workforce preparation. This perspective denies the function of public education as developed in the United States by Horace Mann and others, and harkens back instead to the Middle Ages, when education was provided to the children of successful merchants to "round out" their upbringing. Students in those days were from families whose wealth guaranteed them a good life whether they worked or not; those days are long gone.

"But what of those students who are college-bound?" you may ask. "Certainly they will acquire the necessary work skills in college, and not at the K–12 level." If this were true, we wouldn't have the incredible shortage of highly skilled workers that exists today. Even with the highest college graduation rate in the world, only about 25 percent of U.S. students will graduate from a four-year college, and even fewer will go on to earn advanced degrees. This means that, at minimum, 75 percent of our young people need to leave high school with the requisite skills for today's workplace. And if we just limit our attention to the highly pragmatic list of skills described in this chapter, we can see that they are likely to be as useful to college-bound students as they are to those entering the workforce directly from high school. What college-bound student would not be well-served by being technologically fluent, having good communication skills, working well in teams, demonstrating leadership skills, and being creative and a good problem solver? It seems to me that these skills serve everyone well in today's society, whether they are preparing to enter college or to start a career.

Given the current emphasis on standards-based learning, teachers might well wonder how they're supposed to find the time to teach these essential skills, especially when they are *not* directly addressed on standardized tests. This question is tremendously important, coming as it does from the perspective of those who are still struggling inside Plato's cave. If we go back to the beginning of this chapter, we see how the good (if misguided) intentions of the Business Roundtable came into existence. Rather than focus on the exposition and development of a new curriculum based on the needs of those who will spend their working lives in the 21st century, the Business Roundtable explored ways to improve student performance on the existing subjects using existing tests, without examining whether or not these topics and assessments were germane to the world outside of school. The power of the status quo—of the cave dweller's viewpoint—was so strong that it co-opted the efforts of those who should have known better. Our task is challenging, but not hopeless; at the end of this book we'll explore some concrete strategies for changing educational practice in support of all learners.

7

DIAL LOCALLY, WORK GLOBALLY

The New Global Worker

To many people, the word "globalization" connotes the exploitation of the developing world, the exportation of jobs to lower-wage countries, and a host of other problems that could be fixed if only we locked our borders. While much of the debate has focused on dislocations in the industrial economy, there has not been much discussion of the opportunities globalization provides for the knowledge-value worker.

As the sun sets on our smokestacks, jobs based on the interchangeability of workers are shifting to places where unskilled labor is far cheaper and more abundant than it is in the United States. Because knowledge-value workers are not interchangeable, the effects of globalization are for them quite different. Each knowledge-value worker has a unique approach and creative process that can build cachet and broaden employment opportunities worldwide. Instead of going to the work, as in the Industrial Era, work can now come to the workers—wherever in the world they may be. The consequences of globalization are the exact opposite, for highly skilled knowledge-value workers, of the job losses affecting assembly line workers.

The shift to a knowledge-value economy makes globalization attractive not because it reduces costs, but because it expands opportunities for new business. A growing number of knowledge-value workers now see the entire planet as their market, and are taking advantage of the unprecedented opportunity.

As we explored in Chapter 2, the current Kondratieff wave is expanding opportunities along the edges of the Pacific Rim, Latin America, and China. Couple this with the continued growth of nations affected by previous Kondratieff waves, and it becomes clear that today's knowledge-value worker can secure gainful employment in quite a few countries. Through the use of telematic technologies, this work can even be done without leaving home—so while Industrial-Era jobs are being exported to countries that pay the least, the global knowledge-value worker exports her work to countries where clients pay the most.

Just as rivers, roads, and rails determined the prime locations for factories in the Industrial Era, the availability of glass fibers today determines the location of knowledge work. As broadband wireless networks become commonplace, the entire planet becomes open for unprecedented opportunity. But technology is only part of the equation; you can be the brightest person on the planet, with access to the fastest Internet speeds, and still find your work relegated to a small corner of the globe. The reality is that new markets exist for all kinds of services only if the service providers are aware of and understand regional cultures and languages. Believe it or not, many large corporations have failed to grasp the global opportunities available to them simply because they have ignored the parts of the world that don't speak English.

Language Matters

According to research conducted by WorldLingo.com (2000), over 90 percent of the world's 220 largest companies do not respond to foreign-language e-mail messages, and only about 9 percent of the companies surveyed responded to such messages in the same language as the original e-mail. The worst response rates came from France (0 percent), Japan (0 percent), and Germany (5.5 percent), although the

United Kingdom (16.67 percent), the United States (13.63 percent), and Australia (12.5 percent) were only marginally better. Among the companies that didn't respond at all to foreign-language e-mails were such corporate heavyweights as IBM, AT&T, Intel, Dell Computer (U.S.), BP Amoco (U.K.), Daimler Chrysler (Germany), and Mitsui and Co. (Japan). (If our largest companies can't respond effectively, you can imagine the challenge faced by smaller ventures!) The fastest response came from Morgan Stanley Dean Witter, the U.S. financial services company, which replied in three hours 28 minutes to an e-mail written in Spanish. The second-fastest reply came from the British company AstraZeneca, followed by the U.S. company State Farm Insurance. One U.S. financial services company provided a typical response: "I am in receipt of your e-mail. To forward this to an outside service for interpretation would take several days and not allow us to respond to you in the quickest manner. Can you resubmit your inquiry in English?"

Some people maintain that all we need to do is implement an automated translation into the e-mail loop, so that messages can be quickly converted from one language to another; companies like WorldLingo.com actually perform such services for their clients. The problem is that, except for the most basic correspondence, automated translation of text is problematic. I have looked closely at several programs designed to translate between English and Brazilian Portuguese, and found all of them lacking. To see firsthand how effectively computer translation works, have AltaVista's Babelfish (http://babelfish. altavista.com) translate a paragraph of text from English to another language and back again.

Here's the result of translating the previous paragraph into Brazilian Portuguese and back again to English:

> Some peoples keep that everything that we need to make must execute the translation of machine in the loop of the e-mail in mode that the messages can quickly be converted of a language another one. In the fact, the company as WorldLingo.com executes jobs as this for its customers. The problem is that, to the exception of the most basic correspondence, the translation of machine of the text is problematic. I looked at pròxima in diverse projected programs to translate between the English Portuguese and Brazilian, and to find all to lack. To see, first the hand, as the

71

good computer-translation works, High use Vista.s Babelfish (http://www.altavista.com) and order to translate it another time a paragraph of the text of the English to one another language and have broken back.

By the way, this is one of the better automated translation programs. To be fair, translation is hard. I used a colloquial term—"firsthand"— and these are generally hard to translate. Most languages are loaded with colloquialisms (if your hard drive crashes in Brazil, you might say "The cow went to the swamp"). We need to look at these translation programs as we would a dog walking on its hind legs: we are so surprised to see it doing it at all, we ignore the fact that it doesn't do it well. For the time being, effective translation is still a human task.

Then there's the matter of *cultural* translation. The social graces and business practices of one country are often completely different from those of another. It is only by studying (and preferably living in) cultures other than our own that we can come to appreciate and celebrate these differences. For example, Brazil is a sensual country, and Brazilian Portuguese is a language enhanced by gestures, much like Italian. Brazilians engaged in conversation sit very close to each other, and exchange greetings through the "abraço"—a hug and, often, a kiss on both cheeks. Other countries are more formal: before visiting Japan for the first time, I spent about a half-hour learning how to exchange business cards with my Japanese counterparts. I think it is probably best to learn language and cultural practices at the same time, which has been the approach of every language class I've taken.

If we look at the areas where the economy is likely to grow fastest, we can get a sense of the languages that should be offered to students today:

- English
- Portuguese
- Spanish
- Japanese
- Mandarin
- Korean
- Malay

I'm not trying to slight the other languages; my list is based on guesses as to where the economy will grow the fastest in the next few years. Anyone who knows one foreign language is in a good position, and those with more than one language under their belts will be in great demand over the coming years.

Unfortunately, most schools in the United States save foreign language instruction for high school—at which point a new language is not only harder to acquire, but harder to learn without an accent. If we taught foreign languages from an early age, as is the practice in some other countries, our students would be far better served. In the past, learning another language might not have mattered so much; our economy was so robust and self-contained that most of our citizens could lead very productive lives knowing only English. But today, the more languages you know, the greater your opportunities for success.

The Impact of Globalization

All Business Is Global

There is no question that telematic technologies have accelerated the creation of truly global enterprises. In the past, only the large companies became multinational operations: the General Motors and Hewlett-Packards of the world have long maintained offices, factories, and sales forces in numerous countries. Today, through effective use of the Internet, small businesses have access to global markets and a global talent pool. A venture of almost any size located in the United States can provide products and services globally and contact potential customers through a well-designed Web site. Furthermore, knowledge-value workers can do their work for clients all over the planet without having to physically relocate: an educational software publisher in the United States can e-mail product designs to programmers in Russia, who can then implement the designs and e-mail them back. Payment for services can be done both electronically and through funds transfers. Due to the ease with which nonphysical goods can cross borders, it is increasingly obvious that most business will soon be global in scope.

Even physical products can be transported across borders telematically. Using technologies developed for rapid prototyping, images of complex parts can be sent electronically as a series of instructions for a rapid prototyping device located in another country. As these instructions are received, they tell the fabricating machine exactly how to build a given part, which then emerges, finished, from the machine. These devices can be thought of as three-dimensional fax machines, and they will become less expensive and more versatile as the years progress. The United States already has a specialized version: a Huskvarna Viking Designer Series embroidery machine that can receive complex embroidery patterns over the Internet, copy the data to its disk drive, and then stitch the pattern according to the downloaded instructions. The operator of the machine has only to change the color of the threads when prompted to do so by the sewing machine's display.

Developments like this bring the role of the Industrial Age customs agents into sharp question. The bulk of international commerce is passing through their bodies as wireless data streams while they rummage through suitcases oblivious to the transformations that have already taken place in the mechanisms of global commerce.

It is essential to keep in mind that market competitiveness comes from increased value, not reduced prices. While price pressures may drive physical labor from one country to another, knowledge-value workers can sell their services to the highest bidder, and bid prices will only rise as the bidding pool becomes more and more global.

Distribution of Work

Today's work is increasingly distributed among those best qualified to do it, no matter where they are located. This fact hit home for me one day when I heard Robert Reich talk about globalization: he said that his artificial hip was designed in France and fabricated in Germany. (This was awkward for him, he joked, because as Secretary of Labor, even *he* did not meet "domestic content requirements.") A wired world implies that the best thinkers can collaborate in ways scarcely imaginable a few decades ago.

While the Web and e-mail have served as adequate business tools, they will one day be eclipsed by peer-to-peer work tools that are only just being developed. One of the earliest such systems, Groove.net, allows dispersed work teams to build their own collaborative workspaces. Here they can chat, share documents, arrange calendars, and generally manage complex projects, all from their own computers. Because these tools do not make use of centralized servers (hence the term "peer-to-peer") there is no middleman that can be compromised. Once the application is launched, it immediately checks to see if other team members are online. If they are, the system automatically synchronizes files between team members as they work together. These types of programs will further facilitate the creation of global work teams and the general distribution of labor to the most qualified workers.

Mass Customization

Whether it is an automobile, a computer, or a pair of designer jeans, mass customization is on the rise. As soon as computers were connected to assembly lines, it became easier for each product on the line to be fabricated to specific customer requirements while maintaining the cost advantages associated with mass production. Customer expectations in the world of mass customization are quite high: they will pay a premium to have a product tailored just for them, and will expect it to be delivered in a timely fashion. As a result, manufacturers maintain a very tight loop between the production floor and their suppliers. Warehouses filled with raw parts are being replaced by Intranets that link everyone in the supply chain; this way, when an order comes in, the required components can be brought on site and built into a final product as quickly as possible. Ideally, products are fabricated at the site closest to the customer, to cut down on delivery time. This suggests that small regional factories located near airports will one day become commonplace worldwide. Local fabrication shops can take advantage of locally produced components when possible, and spawn numerous cottage industries in support of the efficient and timely manufacture of customized goods. This may lead to a new type of craft economy, with a global reach made possible by telematics.

If you walk up and down the main street of Passira, Brazil, you'll see lace shops lined up one after another. Lace makers sit in the shade, working on the delicate patterns that will find their way into beautiful linen tablecloths, napkins, bedsheets, and clothing. To the visitor willing to drive several hours from the airport, shopping in Passira is a dream come true: the craftsmanship is incredible, and the prices are fair. What is not apparent at first glance is that the products in this small town are available worldwide. The high-touch world of hand-made fabric masterpieces fits smoothly with the high-tech world of electronic commerce. The lace makers maintain an inventory of common items such as tablecloths, but are also happy to customize their work, making items in specific shapes and sizes as requested by the customer. While the bulk of their work is done by hand, their commerce is conducted with tools as modern as those found in any Fortune 500 company. If these lace makers can be leaders in the global distribution of mass-customized goods, then anyone with a product to sell can do the same.

Work Follows the Sun

When United Airlines loses your baggage, you are given an 800 number to call to check on its location. The last few times my bags were lost in the United States, I've called this number and found that it was being answered in Mexico City. While it seemed strange to be tracking baggage lost on a flight from Chicago to San Francisco through a clerk in Mexico, there are several benefits to having calls answered wherever it is most convenient to do so. The agents in Mexico have access to the same tracking computers as agents in the United States, so they have all the necessary information. My guess is that the decision to have lost baggage calls handled offshore was based on labor costs, but there might be other compelling reasons as well. As commerce becomes increasingly global, telematics allows work to follow the sun: tasks that start in New York in the morning can be moved to San Francisco later in the day, and from there to Hawaii, and on across Asia and Europe as the day progresses. As long as everyone has access to the same information and the requisite skills to address the task, businesses can operate 24 hours a day while staying open no longer than a single work shift per day at any single location. Dun and Bradstreet, for example, uses phone banks located all over the world; most recently I received a routine update call from them that was placed from India.

Knowledge-value work moves at the speed of light and for the ever-diminishing cost of bits. The actual cost of a phone call anywhere in the world via digital transmission is almost zero. Any technology that lets you transport value for nothing was bound to transform the workplace, and telematics already have.

Organic Networks vs. Mechanical Hierarchies

Management in the Industrial Era was based on the model of a military hierarchy, in which successive layers of management take their places along a chain of command leading up to the top decision maker. This model brought stability to vast enterprises with slow- or unchanging infrastructures. As the marketplace started demanding quicker response times from corporations to address the changing needs of consumers, companies with slow-to-respond bureaucracies were at a disadvantage. Globalization further eroded traditional models of management by accelerating the shift from mechanical hierarchies to more fluid systems based on close networks of customers, manufacturers, and suppliers. The decision-making process was moved out of the central office and as close to the customer as possible.

The modern project management structure looks more like a musical jam session in which each player has a chance to solo within a carefully crafted group effort that meets everyone's needs. This style of management system requires that everyone in the chain have core knowledge of the business' goals and direction, as well as the capacity to improvise and make decisions on the fly as demanded by the needs of the local market.

While it is easy to use technology so that everyone at a company has equal access to business information, it is often a challenge for old-line managers to authorize people in the field to act on the company's behalf expeditiously; the "command and control" model of management dies hard. People in the field, such as sales and service managers, need to have enough creativity and trust in their own judgment to make independent decisions based on the best information available.

Where Businesses Locate in the Telematic Age

In mid-2001, several U.S. cities launched an all-out campaign to woo Boeing when the company announced that it was looking for a new home for its corporate headquarters. Denver, Houston, and Chicago made a tremendous effort to entice Boeing, and finally Chicago prevailed; yet the net gain for the destination city was only 500 jobs.

One reason cities work so hard to attract corporations despite the meager returns is image: if one large company moves to an area, others might follow. This type of competition among geographic regions has gone on for many years; many states even maintain offices of which the sole function is to attract businesses from other states. New Mexico and Arizona, for instance, typically set their sights on California companies.

While this attack of the company-snatchers has been largely domestic in scope, it is rapidly becoming international. Powerful global ventures can choose to locate in any of several countries as long as certain infrastructure demands are met. Basically, knowledge-based businesses can relocate to any area with

- Cheap bandwidth

- An international airport

- Access to a skilled workforce

- A high-quality educational system

- Nearby investment capital

- A high quality of life

Cheap bandwidth. Without cheap and reliable bandwidth, today's far-reaching enterprises can't function. The broadband information portal in Recife, Brazil, is a few kilometers from my home, and the transatlantic cable comes ashore about two blocks up the beach from me. I can get Internet access at two million bits per second for about $20 (U.S.) per month. Contrast this with the complete lack of broadband at my Ameritech-served home in the United States, and you'll find one of the reasons I like working in Brazil.

An international airport. Because physical mobility is important, local access to an international airport is important. Any area within an hour's drive to the airport is ideal.

Access to a skilled workforce. Obviously, you'll need a local workforce as an employment pool if you are building a local operation of any size, but it is important even if you will be a sole practitioner, as these are the people who will form part of your local "nutrient broth" for ideas. You'll want to tap into their expertise and insights, just as they will want to tap into yours. It is hard to stay abreast of any field if you are physically isolated from others who share your interests.

A high-quality educational system (including a university or two). These institutions not only provide a pool of highly skilled workers, but also a demand for local cultures that support lifelong learning.

Nearby investment capital. The sole practitioner may not need investment capital, but it sure is comforting to know that it's around. Investment bankers and venture firms tend to attract bright people with interesting ideas; they make interesting lunch companions even if you don't seek their money.

A high quality of life. Finally, the cultural and recreational aspect of a community is essential in attracting businesses. I love Chicago for its museums, symphony, and blues clubs; even if I don't go into town every week, it's nice to know that these resources are there when I want them. When I'm in Recife, we go out almost every weekend to enjoy the local music and great food. Beyond that, every morning I can walk out my front door and cross the street for a walk along one of the most beautiful beaches in the world. The high-touch aspects of a community are just as important as the high-tech aspects when looking for a place to do business.

The New Nomads

I'm encountering more and more people who lead nomadic lifestyles, maintaining homes in more than one location. It is not uncommon to find someone with two primary residences located in countries where their business interests are the strongest, and who then also has one or more vacation residences elsewhere.

Although our work and customers may be global, we all need a physical home location in which to live, have our families, and interact with friends. Not too many years ago, it was common to meet people whose families lived in the same general location for generations. The Thornburg family, for example, had a large cluster in and around Muncie, Indiana; in fact, several businesses in Muncie carry the Thornburg family name, and I still encounter previously unknown relatives every time I visit. My father broke away and moved all the way to Chicago, where he spent the bulk of his life. I carried on the wanderlust tradition, relocating after college to the San Francisco Bay area, and then back to Chicago, but at the same time also moving to Recife, Brazil. My son, Harvey, will possibly end up living in Belgium, or some other country, once he finishes his Ph.D.; one of our daughters lives in São Paulo, Brazil, and the other is attending college in Recife after completing high school in the United States.

What about family? What about roots? Don't these things matter any more? Well, of course they do—it's just that many of us are able to establish multiple roots fairly easily, and we take comfort in knowing that members of our family are just a plane ride away. When splitting your home between two countries, the challenge lies not only in dealing with two languages, but also in developing two sets of friends and of local places to enjoy. One way my family has found to keep both cultures alive at all times is to arrange for Brazilian television as part of our satellite service in the United States; some North American stations are already available through our Brazilian cable system. This way, no matter where we are, we hear both English and Portuguese on a daily basis. And thanks to e-mail and inexpensive telephone calls, we are always in contact with those we care about, no matter where they (or we) might be.

Successful multinational workers should become immersed in the culture of their adopted countries. Rather than just hanging out with the expatriate community, it is essential to become deeply connected to the local scene. When we are in Brazil, I'm surrounded by Portuguese speakers; I eat (and love!) Brazilian food; I hang out in local music clubs; and, in the spirit of the country, I even dance in the Brazilian streets.

While the nomadic life may not suit everyone, it is becoming more common as global commerce expands. But even if you don't plan on having more than one residence, it is essential that you resist a parochial view of your home country. This can be done in several ways—by subscribing to an international news magazine published outside the United States, for instance, like *The Economist* of Great Britain, or by watching television shows from other countries. I myself enjoy watching foreign television ads because they give a quick snapshot of products that appeal to other societies, and the imagery used in the ads provides a window into their popular culture. News broadcasts are also worth watching—especially when they are about events happening in the United States! Finally, the common language of sports (in our house, soccer) gives you a sense of the connectedness of nations around a common theme. As a U.S. citizen, I came to appreciate soccer as a slower version of ice hockey with fewer fights. (As a result, I'm trying to get my Brazilian friends interested in hockey!) Many foreign newspapers and radio stations have Web sites, so even those without cable or satellite television can dip their toes into other cultures on a regular basis. To me, one of the greatest benefits of living in two countries is that I think differently when I change locations: I find I do my most creative work when I'm in Brazil, and my most analytical when I'm in the United States.

No matter where on earth you may choose to work, it is crucial to realize that your children are likely to have opportunities to work anywhere in the world they want, and that they will likely thrive as multinational citizens of Earth in ways we can hardly imagine.

8

THE NEW WORK

Imagine you could travel back in time—to the 1960s perhaps—and attend a dinner party. As a time traveler from the 21st century, you might describe some of the gadgets you commonly use. Imagine discussing the popularity of e-mail, DVDs, digital cameras, or any of the other devices advertised in today's newspapers. How would the guests respond? At the very least they would be amazed, and most likely they wouldn't believe what you told them. The fact is, for my generation at least, the transformations we've seen stagger the imagination. And just as our gadgets have changed, so have our industries: the author and presenter Joel Barker (1992) says that "Made in Japan" used to signify junk; now it implies high quality. The continued growth of multi-national companies has carried with it the demand for a multinational force of skilled workers whose organizational chart looks more like a web than a hierarchy. Some companies that were high on the Fortune 500 list in the 1960s are now either defunct or have merged with other ventures to stay alive. Who could have anticipated that the Sabre software developed by American Airlines for a national ticket reserva-tion system would now be worth more than the airline itself?

As amazing as these changes are, they will pale in comparison with the changes we will see in the coming years. I can say this with some certainty, even if I don't know the specifics of the future, because the development and adoption of new ideas and products is a highly nonlinear process that leads to complex chaotic behavior. For example, the microprocessor chip was an outgrowth of a project designed to allow the creation of inexpensive calculators. Viewed from this perspective, the microprocessor was seen only as an amalgamation of thousands of components that would otherwise occupy a large and expensive circuit board; the chip was initially seen as a cost-reduction strategy for an existing product line. However—and here is where things get interesting—hobbyists and others saw the potential of this chip to let them make their own computers. At the time, no existing computer manufacturers had shown any interest in these devices. Instead, they saw their industry continuing on a linear growth path and focused on the needs of their existing customers. In the meantime, the hobbyist computer movement represented a nonlinear diversion of an existing technology that started to spawn new companies, which in turn built computers from microprocessors. Companies like Tandy, Apple, Commodore, and many others entered the market years before IBM, CDC, and other "real" computer companies could even see what was happening. The complex and chaotic creation of a major new segment of the economy was unforeseen, yet has grown to touch all of our lives.

As the above example shows, rather than evolve in a linear extrapolation from the past, new ideas or technologies sometimes develop that transform industries in ways their inventors could never have predicted. We call these new technologies "wild cards" because they are incredibly powerful and can't be anticipated in advance. The author Clayton Christensen (1997) calls them "disruptive technologies" because they can disrupt the status quo virtually overnight.

"Wild Card" Technologies of the Past

When the transistor was discovered at Bell Labs in the 1940s, no one could have anticipated the impact it would have on our lives today. (Note that I said the transistor was discovered, not invented. The three researchers who discovered a useful application of the device were conducting basic research on semiconductor physics, not trying to "invent" a new product!) From a single lab experiment, the transistor went on to become the most prolific item of mass production in history.

Every era has had its share of wild cards: the telegraph, telephone, transistor, personal computer, ATM, microwave oven, and VCR have each changed, in some way, our behavior, lifestyle, or workplace. One of the few institutions that have escaped relatively unscathed by the disruptive technologies of the past 50 years is "school." By and large, schools have avoided change by ignoring, banning, or trying to co-opt new technologies. Only the personal computer and the Internet are now starting to have an impact. The fact remains that our great-grandparents could walk into most of today's classrooms and recognize almost everything they see.

I have no idea what the jobs of the future will be, or even what industries will be the strongest (although I have some candidates). And I'm not alone in my uncertainty; no one has an accurate crystal ball for the next 50 years, in part because our economic system is not linear enough to allow those kinds of forecasts. The only certainty is change. The challenge for educational institutions is to prepare their students for the years to come without knowing exactly what the future holds.

The first key is to look, as we have, at foundational skills that can be applied across the board in virtually any industry. Second, by promoting lifelong learning as the only effective coping strategy for change, we can build resiliency in those who may hop from career to career several times during their working years.

Three Current Trends

Looking for the moment at current trends, some areas seem to hold great promise in the coming years. By exploring some of these we can, perhaps, get a glimmer of disruptions that may mature into full-fledged industries by the time our children graduate from school.

Although the following trends are not new, they are still at an early stage of development: information technology, bioinformatics, and bioethics. You may be surprised that I've chosen these three trends in particular. After all, information technology has been with us for quite some time—long enough for stocks to rise to the sky and then tumble back to earth. As some might say, "That is *so* last century!" Yet there are enough surprises in store for us in this sector to convince me that it will continue to grow in the years to come.

Information Technology

The recent development of peer-to-peer applications that break the hierarchy of the client-server model typified by traditional Web sites is one of these surprises. Napster, for example, became the fastest growing Internet application of all time simply because it allowed music files stored on each user's computer to be shared with others automatically. Because Napster was not a true peer-to-peer application—it maintained a central directory of files that could be downloaded—its "pressure point" was exposed, allowing it to be crippled by a lawsuit from the recording industry. In the meantime, true peer-to-peer file sharing programs such as Gnutella and its offspring are virtually immune from attack, and are a serious threat to the status quo. Other peer-to-peer applications designed to promote collaboration, solve complex biochemical problems, and even help in the search for life in other corners of the Universe are coming into use on a regular basis. The initial chaotic flurry around Napster clouded the deeper significance of these kinds of programs: they change the way we think about the Internet, and open the door to new ways of working and communicating with each other.

As long as we can still be surprised by developments in this area, information technology is still in the early stages of its potential, both in terms of hardware and software. Although the Internet started out as a way for people to communicate and share ideas with each other, it is increasingly being used to allow automated systems to interact. The Ceiva picture frame, for example, allows pictures to be automatically downloaded from a special Web address without human intervention. It is possible that the dominant traffic on the Internet will soon be between computers that run without direct human involvement.

Bioinformatics and Bioethics

Genetic research received a lot of attention in the first year of this century when the human genome was mapped and found to be less complex than anticipated. One of the many technologies that played a role in this project was the "gene chip," which allows the activity of thousands of genes to be determined overnight at low cost. This chip, made by Affymetrix, uses single strand fragments of DNA to isolate particular genes from a solution made out of a test sample. Each gene is attracted to a strand fragment with which it is associated, allowing up to 20,000 or so genes to be analyzed at the same time. Prior to the invention of this chip, it could take up to six months and cost $100,000 to do the work that can be done today overnight for about $100.

The gene chip is valuable at present for research, and will likely emerge as a diagnostic tool for diseases ranging from breast cancer to HIV. Diagnostic tools with this power will have an incredible impact on medicine, because they can allow the proclivity of certain ailments to be detected prior to the onset of disease. As we come to know more about the genetic nature of certain illnesses, gene-specific therapies are likely to be developed that can block, forever, the triggering of a disease-causing gene. This proactive approach to medical practice will possibly change the way medical doctors do their work.

The future may also bring back a practice common to doctors a hundred years ago—the preparation of their own medicines. My great grandfather's medical kit was filled with numerous compounds and a detailed notebook on the proper blends of the chemicals needed to treat different ailments. In the future, your doctor might have a special ink-jet printer that sprays a blend of the exact prescription onto special paper tabs, to be placed under the tongue for absorption into the bloodstream. If this were to happen, the role of the corner pharmacist might also be redefined.

Speaking of genes, think about those people for whom tests reveal the possibility of a certain disease that has yet to emerge. How should the doctor deal with that information, especially if there is no known cure? This leads to another field of endeavor that will likely grow in the future: bioethics. In 2001, bioethicists had to deal with the use of stem cells and the continued controversy surrounding cloning. In the future, however, their plates will be full with many other challenges.

The one characteristic of the three fields mentioned so far is that they all require high levels of skill and are tailor-made for people whose interests span more than one discipline. Bioinformatics, for example, involves both biochemistry and computer skills. If we think the educational requirements for today's jobs are demanding, especially in math and science, the jobs of the future will require expanding both the breadth and depth of our skills.

Just as we have a current shortage of IT workers, shortages will appear in other fields as well, especially those requiring high levels of skill. Once again, this reinforces the need for schools to continue their efforts to develop and maintain student interest and enthusiasm for challenging subjects.

Transforming the Trades

Of course, the continued growth in the need for highly skilled knowledge workers doesn't mean that manual labor is dead. While it is true that mindless assembly-line jobs will continue to be automated or outsourced to nations with a surplus of low-skill, low-wage laborers, independent contract tradespeople will always be in high demand. Electricians, carpenters, plumbers, painters, farmers, and others will continue to thrive. It would be a mistake, however, to refer to these people as low-skilled workers. Because tradespeople have historically operated as independent contractors, they are as eager to use telematic tools in support of their craft as any large corporation. Landscapers, for example, will often sit down with a potential client and sketch a rough plan for a garden on a laptop computer, and then show color images of flowers that go with the decor of the house. As plants are chosen, they can be placed on the virtual plot so the client can see, roughly, what the garden will look like when it is finished. Similarly, caterers and party planners use technology to coordinate events.

Farmers are probably among the most advanced users of technology. A few years ago I had dinner with a farmer in central Illinois. I used to work on a ranch many years ago, so I asked what the greatest advance in farming had been since the days when I was (literally) in the field. Without hesitation he said, "gene splicing." Now when I worked on a ranch, jeans were something you wore, not something you "spliced." The farmer was referring to the development of herbicide-resistant, genetically modified soybeans that could survive even the strongest weed killers. As he went into his discussion of exactly how the gene splice worked, I found my knowledge of biochemistry stretched to the limit. At that point I thought it would be great if every child graduating from high school could carry on an intelligent conversation with a farmer.

With the increased use of telematics in virtually every work sector, there will be a growing need for technicians in all areas of electronic technology. While many of these high-paying jobs do not require college degrees, they all require some education beyond high school, as well as continuous lifelong learning.

My friend Bob Hughes used to say that all wealth was generated from the neck up; everything from the neck down was minimum wage. Today, minimum-wage jobs are in countries other than the United States. Modern manual workers are highly skilled craftspeople who use their brains much more than they probably admit.

There is an apocryphal story about the great engineer and scientist Nikola Tesla, who developed the alternating current generator. One day, Tesla was called to a power generating plant where the generator was running at very low speed. He saw that the flywheel was out of alignment, so he took a hammer and as the wheel rotated to the right position, tapped it slightly to spring it back into place. The generator quickly came to full speed, and the problem was solved.

"How much do I owe you?" the plant manager asked.

"Five dollars and fifty cents," Tesla replied.

"Five fifty for hitting a wheel with a hammer?"

"No sir," said Tesla. "For hitting the wheel, the charge is fifty cents. The five dollars were for knowing *where* to hit it."

We may not know what jobs will be commonplace in the coming years, but we can be certain that they will all involve "knowing where to hit the wheel."

9

THE NEW SCHOOL

In this book I have referred to the specific content areas and skills that every person needs in order to be a productive member of the economy. My emphasis has been on describing those skills that have long-term value, and that hopefully will last a lifetime—and, thus, should be taught in school.

Whether you are a teacher, a student, a parent, or other member of your community, I want you to measure your schools using the scoring boxes provided in Figure 9.1. Place a check mark in the box that best describes how effectively your school addresses the topic. Be as honest in your assessment as possible; if you are in doubt about some of these items, ask your children what they think. Once you've completed this task, we'll examine what steps, if any, are needed to align your school with these attributes. If you find that your school scores highly in all areas, then you can take comfort in the fact that students will likely be getting the background they need to thrive in the coming years.

Clearly, if your schools are not scoring as highly as they might, you need to start a dialogue with educational leaders in your area to help create a climate of change. Remember that classroom teachers are generally among the most dedicated, hard-working professionals you'll ever encounter. If they are not addressing the needs of their students, it might be because they don't know what skills today's workers

Figure 9.1
CHECKING OUT YOUR SCHOOLS

Decide whether students complete school exhibiting mastery of each of the skills listed. Place a check mark to show whether all, some, or none of the students achieve each given skill.

All	Some	None	Skill
			Abstraction
			Systems thinking
			Experimentation
			Collaboration
			Comfort with ambiguity
			Lifelong learning
			Creativity
			Entrepreneurship
			Viewing history as process, not "facts"
			Nonlinear math, especially chaos and complexity
			Improvisation
			Technological fluency
			Communications (including public-speaking and presentation-design skills)
			Leadership
			Problem solving
			Valuing cultural diversity
			Pride in work
			Knowledge of the humanities and arts
			One or two foreign languages, including Portuguese, Spanish, Japanese, Mandarin, Korean, Malay

Place a check mark below to show whether all, some, or none of the students are taught by teachers exhibiting these characteristics.

			Teachers expert in their disciplines (e.g., math, science)
			Teachers instill passion for their subjects
			Teachers hold high expectations for their students
			Teachers maintain curriculum focus on "long-life" skills

require. If this is the case, you might want to host a discussion group on the topics explored in this book. Perhaps the teachers feel so encumbered by traditional classroom practice and the increased pressure of standardized testing that they can't see a clear way to radically change their teaching methods or curriculum. In this situation, teachers need a deeper well of support in order to make the necessary changes. In still other cases, the challenge may lie with administrators who are not providing the kind of in-depth support needed to reframe educational practice in their schools. Conversations centered on the topics in this book may guide people to craft a new vision of schools that supports of children more effectively.

Above all, remember that the educators in your community are not your enemies, but rather strong supporters of your children's needs. Unfortunately, they often lack the resources and support needed to effect change—which breeds frustration that can turn to anger or despondency. Anyone who wants to make fundamental changes in the classroom needs to develop a plan and obtain the support needed to bring the plan to fruition. By keeping the needs of our students in the public mind—through newspaper articles, speeches at open houses, etc.—educators can get the kind of support they need to make these deep changes. (I'll have more to say about this in the last chapter of this book.)

Characteristics of the New School

When thinking about schools for the 21st century, two fundamental characteristics come to mind: that learning is contextual; and that school is a process, not a place.

Learning Is Contextual

If we examine Sakaiya's theories about the evolution of labor through history (as described in Chapter 4) in terms of education, we can glean the following insights. Learning in the time of the guilds was highly contextualized. Stonemasons learned their trade by being apprenticed to masters, who would work with them over the years to develop their skills. Apprenticeships took place on the worksite; once proficient, young masons could start adding their own stones to constructions in progress. Because one person was responsible for a complete stone (or other craft item) in this era, work was contextualized—and, hence, so was learning.

The industrial age decontextualized work. Now the worker was on an assembly line and responsible for only one part of a finished product. When Eli Whitney invented the assembly line concept for the manufacture of rifles, his goal was to allow workers with minimal skills to quickly produce quality products that would have taken a single craftsman a long time to complete. When Henry Ford adopted Whitney's concepts to the manufacture of automobiles, the decontextualization of work had become the norm. At the same time that work was being decontextualized in factories, the same was happening to education. Students were clustered by age, and subjects were taught in isolation from each other. Just as bells and whistles controlled the flow of work on the factory floor, bells and "scope and sequence" mandates controlled the flow of information at school. Students were taught and then assessed to see what they had retained. An educated student was seen as the successful "product" of a school, to be graduated at the end of the educational assembly line. Much like their industrial counterparts, teachers only worked on one aspect of a student's learning at a time, dividing them up either by subject or by age.

Much of this decontextualized approach to education is still in place, even as corporations move toward the realities of the Knowledge-Value Era. For the knowledge-value worker, *everything* is highly contextual; information devoid of context is meaningless. Just as our schools mirrored the dominant paradigm of decontextualization during the industrial era, they must now reshape themselves to mirror the needs of the knowledge-value worker. But unlike the guild-based model of education, in which each apprentice must learn the limited skills necessary for a particular career, today's knowledge-value workers must learn a variety of skills in order to shift seamlessly from one career to another throughout their working years. The recontextualization of learning needs to take place within a completely new framework for education; deep systemic changes are needed, both in subject matter and teaching methods.

It seems to me that one of the easiest ways to recontextualize learning is to focus on student projects, and preferably long-term ones. A sufficiently complex project will provide opportunities for students to explore every subject area within the context of a single theme. For example, take a look at the lesson guide for the Mars Millennium Project (2000), a joint venture of the U. S. Department of Education, NASA, the Getty Foundation, and others. The project challenges students to design habitable communities for placement on Mars in 2030. In order to design a community, students need to explore math, science, social studies, arts, and the whole spectrum of subjects normally taught in school. Unlike traditional instruction, however, the Mars project binds these subjects together within the context of a central theme, and encourages students to "pull" information from teachers as needed, rather than having it "pushed" onto them in the manner of decontextualized education.

"Jamming" as a Pedagogical Model

A refinement of project-based learning that is worth exploring is based on something blues and jazz musicians do all the time—"jamming." As discussed in Chapter 4, this is when musicians join together in spontaneous improvisation around a common theme. Musicians who've never even met before will often get together for the first time in front of a large audience and play off of each other, interpreting beautifully a number that was never played that way before and will not be played that way again. While commonly associated with music, the principles of jamming can also be applied to the study of academic subjects by leading to new ways of approaching a problem that take everyone by surprise. Jamming can be applied to many classroom subjects, just as musicians jam around many musical forms (in my college days I even jammed with friends on themes by Bach!). And just as most musicians jam on musical themes using instruments, learners can jam on academic themes using technology, especially with peer-to-peer systems like Groove.net.

Key Elements of a Jam Session

Jamming requires more than one person. Even if you are jamming to a prerecorded piece of music, it took others to set the background for your improvisation.

Jamming follows rules. Musicians need to agree on the key, tempo, and overall structure of the piece of music that will serve as the framework for the session.

Everyone helps everyone else. I was listening to a jazz performance one day in which the trumpet player had migrated into the wrong key. The sax player came to the rescue by playing a harmonizing riff—a melodic fragment that moved into the trumpet player's key and gently led him back home (to the astounded delight of the audience).

Everyone gets to solo. While the overall process involves group collaboration, each member is expected to contribute a unique element that requires everyone else to pick up on the lead and follow it wherever it goes.

Jamming goes to new places. The creativity involved in improvisation in a group setting virtually guarantees that new ideas will emerge that the members would not have thought of on their own.

Jamming builds rapport. Every time my blues band—the Bluesmen of the Silicon Delta—gets together for rehearsal, we spend some time just "noodling around." These free-form jam sessions have led to new riffs that we incorporate in our performances, and have even resulted in a new song or two. The ease with which we collaborate is reflected in our personal relationships as well: when you jam with someone, you know that person in a deep way.

There are other rules, I'm sure, but the ones above can set the stage for learning-centered jamming. My guess is that any teacher would be happy if, in addition to learning their lessons, students worked well as a group, followed rules carefully, helped other classmates while exhibiting their own creativity, explored topics in a new way, and built rapport with other students. In other words, the teacher would be happy if the students jammed.

An academic jam session would begin with a topic, such as the battle of New Orleans. To get started, everyone in the group would need to know the original "piece"; once everyone is up to speed on the basic facts, the team can start to jam with ideas related to this event. For example, this tragic battle was fought after the war was over. Why did it happen? What role did communication technology play? Could it ever happen again? Such questions could form the basis of academic "riffs" that each member of the team might expand upon in turn, with the rest of the team providing backup during solos. Finally, the team would want to create a final "performance" of its session—perhaps exploring the battle of New Orleans from the perspective of people on both sides of the conflict. The important point is that there is no hard and fast formula for creating a jam session; each group in a class might approach the same topic from a completely different point of view. What they would have in common is a solid grounding in the topic, and the ability to extend their knowledge themselves through collaboration.

School as a Process, Not a Place

The idea that learning is an anywhere, anytime, lifelong process flies in the face of schooling models based on buildings that are open only several hours a day for a number of months a year. While home-based computing is on the rise, this still does not provide true access to information at all places and times. The technology that seems closest to meeting that need in the next few years is that of powerful handheld computers such as the Compaq iPaq or the Palm OS devices. By mid-2001, products like the iPaq were already supporting completely wireless Web access and were able to play rich media files (including full-length feature films). The formats of these devices are already comfortable to children weaned on the Nintendo GameBoy. One challenge faced by users of these devices is that of high-resolution output. This will probably be addressed in time through a head-mounted display, similar to the Olympus Eye Trek. This device looks like a pair of glasses but contains two full-color retinal projectors, one for each eye, that create an image similar to that of a 21-inch video screen.

While still somewhat expensive and not easily connected to a palm-sized computer, there is little question that devices like this can provide unprecedented opportunities for anywhere, anytime learning.

I like to think of the pedagogy supported by these devices as "trickle learning" since students can use their handheld computers at odd moments of the day—during bus rides, waiting for doctor appointments, etc. To use these tools effectively, students need to be able to start and stop their activities at a moment's notice without losing their place, so the devices need to be as easy to interrupt as a book is with a bookmark. In addition, teachers must design activities for students that take into account the new technology—especially since, unlike traditional classrooms, trickle learners may have anywhere from minutes to hours available for their lessons. This kind of variability fits in quite well in the context of student-directed project-based learning. For example, a student doing field work for a history project can conduct research online while visiting a historic site, and can even send information to others in the project who may be working on a different aspect of the research. True "anytime, anywhere" computing holds great promise for all learners at any age.

The greatest challenge in crafting the new school is going to be human, not technological. We need to examine the validity of assumptions that have remained unchallenged for generations. Parents, board members, administrators, educators, and students will all need to adapt to new curriculum and teaching methods. Fortunately, some schools have already taken the lead in making these changes, and they can share their experiences with those preparing for the journey ahead. As hard as the trip may be, the results will be worth the effort. At the very least, we will have transformed schools that taught *some* students at *some* locations *some* subjects at *some* time into environments that allow every learner to learn about anything, anywhere, at anytime.

10

A ROLE FOR GOVERNMENTS
IN THE NEW ECONOMY

The policies of most governments in the world tend to lag behind changes in the needs of business and education. Elected officials often appear to be either unaware or insensitive to the changes necessary for their people to thrive. This is particularly evident in regard to education. Virtually every elected official wants quality education for its populace, but often supports mandates that inadvertently reinforce the status quo rather than foster deep systemic change (e.g., improved scores on standardized tests). It is easy, then, to see why some are calling for the privatization of education, on the assumption that market forces alone can result in the educational systems we need. Unfortunately, most private schools seem no better equipped to prepare students for the future than do our public institutions.

Profound systemic change can take years to take effect, and its benefits are often not evident in time for reelection. This fosters a desire on the part of politicians for a quick fix: a silver bullet that, combined with a few photo opportunities, will make the official appear to take education seriously.

Government and Testing

As mentioned previously, the rush is on to implement high-stakes multiple-choice testing in schools. Officials who have no idea what questions students will be asked on exams continue to clamor for higher test scores, as if this could possibly measure how prepared our students are for life after school. The strongest proponents of these tests seem to never have seen them, or to have any interest in seeing them. This problem runs all the way down to individual school districts, and results in such idiocy as the promises by state governors not to rest until all the children in their states score above average!

If you want to get a room full of superintendents so quiet you can hear a pin drop, just announce, as I have, that you're passing out a page from their local high-school test for them to take and grade. You can practically hear the sweat drip onto the floor. Whenever I conduct this experiment, I ask the superintendents why they're so afraid of taking the test; their response, usually, is that they don't think they'll do too well on it. I then point out that they are successful in life, so why should the test bother them? The response I often get is that the tests do not measure things related to success in life. When I ask why they give the tests to students, the superintendents respond that the government makes us give the tests. I have tried to track down congressmen to see if they are willing to take the tests, but have found no takers.

So here is my first suggestion for government: place a moratorium on all standardized tests until they can be evaluated against a list of skills needed for success in the coming years. Both the content and methodology of the examination need to be evaluated. For example, multiple-choice exams are used in only two places outside of school that I know of: driver's license exams and certain TV game shows. Any test of a student's capabilities needs to be contextual, as it is in the world outside of school. Officials who persist in calling for standardized tests should first have to take the test themselves and have their scores published in the newspapers. (This probably would end this type of testing overnight.)

Since I try to be a realist from time to time, I won't hold my breath waiting for these ideas to be adopted. Instead, parents and concerned educators need to take matters into their own hands. For example, your state may allow parents to opt their students out of these mindless examinations. Parental boycotts are another option. The Web site PencilsDown.org is a good starting place for information on the testing movement.

Please note that I am not against measuring student achievement. I just think that these measurements need to be contextual in order to be relevant to life in the telematic age.

Government and Restructuring Education

In addition to damping the testing mania, government can help to actually restructure education. Most schools, both public and private, operate according to an agrarian-age calendar and an Industrial-Age pedagogical model. The fact that our grandparents would recognize virtually every aspect of today's schools should shame us into making the radical transformations that the needs of our students demand. The schools of the past were created for an economic era driven by the needs of industry, not knowledge-value workers.

There are two main reasons that government should help transform our schools. First, most children go to public schools, which are run by the government. Second, failure to transform education will adversely impact the long-term economic future of any nation, and this most certainly should be of concern to government.

Government and Trade

While tariffs slow internal development and keep local companies from developing products of value to the global market, vast amounts of valuable data can and do flow across borders tax-free in the form of diaphanous bits. Anything that can be expressed in digital form can be sent at tremendous speed through the glass fibers and satellite data feeds encircling the globe. Bits can represent text, sounds, movies, and even money; in short, anything that provides high value in the Knowledge-Value Era. Bits can't be seen and can barely be counted. While customs inspectors assess duties on physical products that cross their borders, information of far greater value is traveling back and forth by telematic means.

In attempting to protect local industries, tariffs often block access to advanced technologies that countries need to transform their economies. This is especially evident in the rapidly growing field of information technology. Many countries have a sufficiently skilled cadre of IT workers to jump-start their local economy, but lack the sophisticated hardware and software needed to support these efforts. The obvious solution is to acquire this technology from countries that already have it. Vendors worldwide are actively searching for new markets; unfortunately, so-called protective tariffs in some countries may act to impede rather than enhance the very economy they are designed to protect. This well-intentioned holdover from the Industrial Age can be devastating in the telematic era of today.

Government and Immigration

Just as the global economy benefits from free trade, local economies benefit from an influx of highly skilled workers. As mentioned previously in this book, we do not have nearly enough high-skill workers to meet current job demands, and yet it is quite difficult to bring such workers in from other countries. Furthermore, today's knowledge-value workers are likely to operate from a global stage and to bring value both to their home countries, where they pay taxes and spend money, and to the client country, where their services help local economic growth. As mentioned before, those who cling to the idea that we are still in the Industrial Age see globalization as a threat. But in the current era, globalization provides increased opportunity for everyone, and this opportunity is enhanced when governments make it easier for people to move across borders and live and work in other countries.

Some fear that freer immigration will lead to hordes of people at our shores that will drain our resources. The perception is that the economy is a zero-sum game, with only so many jobs to go around. The problem with this scenario is that it denies the reality of the Knowledge-Value Era: opportunity and growth come from the minds of the people, and the more highly skilled people a country has, the better off it is likely to be.

Current immigration policy in the United States makes it very difficult for someone to set up residency here. It can take years to get a green card, and without the aid of an immigration lawyer, the applicant is at the constant mercy of the INS, who seems to treat applicants as though they were criminals. For example, if a highly skilled multinational worker is applying for residency in the United States and, during this process, needs to travel to other countries, she must first apply for and be granted a "parole." The worker is then identified officially as an "alien on parole," and is subjected to additional paperwork every time she returns to the United States. Furthermore, the interview process required to secure parole and other changes in status are designed to bury the applicant in fees and paperwork and are often conducted in a humiliating manner. It is little wonder, then, that many who wish to live in the United States simply skip the formal application process and live their lives as undocumented aliens, holding down minimum-wage, all-cash jobs to avoid a paper trail. In my view, the INS should either be scrapped or required to hire only Native Americans, since everyone else in this country is either an immigrant or related to immigrants.

While some fear that the United States will be overrun with alien Ph.D.s and other highly skilled immigrants, the fact is that countries experiencing a brain drain of their own workers will be forced to entice them back. This is already happening in Malaysia, where the export of skilled workers is making it difficult for local companies to find new employees with the requisite skills. In response to this problem, Malaysia is asking expatriate workers in other countries to come home, and sweetening the pot with reduced taxes and other incentives.

From the perspective of employers, immigration quotas simply serve to increase the number of foreign workers who stay in their home countries and telecommute. From the perspective of an enlightened and self-interested government, it would make sense to let these workers emigrate, so that they could pay taxes in the country for which they work. I am a U.S. citizen, and I'm proud of my country. But I'm also a multinational worker whose work (I hope) benefits both the United States and any country for which I work. As telematics-enhanced globalization of the economy proceeds, it becomes increasingly apparent that many countries, including the United States, need to revise their immigration policies.

Government and Communications Infrastructure

Infrastructure investments in support of interstate commerce are, I think, properly seen as requiring the support of the federal government. In the past, the government invested in canals and in the interstate highway system. Many years ago, a small government-funded project set the stage for a new infrastructure in need of development: the Internet. Telecommunication companies provide the physical hardware—the cables, bridges, and routers—necessary for development, and the standards that ensure interoperability on networks are these days international in scope.

Near the beginning of this book I explored the challenge of standards: on the one hand they inhibit creativity, but on the other they guarantee interoperability. Standards change over time, and new standards inevitably replace old ones. Countries that are just now moving into the telematic era have the advantage of being able to adopt the latest standards, because there is little or no installed base of older technology to render obsolete. This phenomenon is most evident with cell phones. Many countries, including Japan and Brazil, have cell phones with features unavailable in the United States because U.S. cell phone usage grew tremendously before the latest standards were established. This fact suggests that governments should keep an eye open for emerging global standards that might benefit their citizens, and encourage the adoption of new standards when appropriate.

In addition to communication standards, governments all the way down to the local level need to ensure that no communities are left behind in terms of access to communication technology. We wouldn't think of building a city without access to a main highway, yet many parts of the country are digital wastelands with no access to broadband communication at a reasonable cost. The onus, in this case, falls on the local government to rectify this situation. In the telematic age, access to broadband is a starting point, not a goal. Communities like mine in the suburbs of Chicago are rapidly being left behind. For example, even though our residential community houses people well above the 90th percentile in national income, we consider ourselves lucky if we get reliable telephone service. As for DSL or any other broadband services provided by telephone companies, they are unavailable at any price, despite our proximity to a local switch. Cable modems are not available, and a cheap broadband wireless service used in Chicago lies just outside our range. My only option is to have my own broadband satellite link, which is like taking a sledgehammer to a thumbtack.

My point in sharing this story is not to vent my anger at the local telephone company—they get enough phone calls from me as it is—but to point out that "redlining," the process of denying service to certain communities, is not just a problem for the poor but affects those at both ends of the economic spectrum. The solution to this problem seems fairly simple. Telephone service requires communities to grant easements in order for wires to reach homes and businesses, and these wires need to be buried and run across multiple property lines. If local governments chose only to provide easements to carriers willing to bring a full spectrum of reasonably priced services to all corners of a community, you can be sure that these services would be offered.

Please do not infer from the above that I support greater government control over our lives; I agree with Thomas Jefferson's assertion that he who governs least, governs best. Having said that, there are two distinct challenges governments face in our new era. First, policies that impede global economic forces need to be overhauled or scrapped. Second, those areas that benefit from government funding, such as education and infrastructure easements, need to be transformed in ways that support the new economy. The blind implementation of outdated policies and laws runs the risk of leading us toward economic decline.

11

THE CAVE REVISITED

As we come to the close of our journey into the future of work, you may find yourself in the delicate position of enlightening those who are still in the cave of current educational practice. As Plato has warned, don't expect a warm welcome; some will find your message very threatening. Machiavelli summed it up nicely in *The Prince* when he wrote:

> It ought to be remembered that there is nothing more difficult to take in hand, more perilous to conduct, or more uncertain in its success, than to take the lead in the introduction of a new order of things. Because the innovator has for enemies all those who have done well under the old conditions, and lukewarm defenders in those who may do well under the new. This coolness arises partly from fear of the opponents, who have the laws on their side, and partly from the incredulity of men, who do not readily believe in new things until they have had a long experience of them.

In this chapter I'll share some ideas on how to help your community effect the transformations you'll need in order to ensure that every student is equipped to thrive in the telematic economy.

Change Is a Community Effort

The transformations described in this book cannot be implemented without the full support and understanding of the entire community. School districts that implement radical changes independent of the community are prone to high levels of criticism—usually accompanied by the firing of the superintendent and other key executives in the school system. Communities often react strongly because there is no common base of understanding among all parties involved; remember that most community members think of education in terms of their own school experiences, and will consequently question any radical changes to the model of their youth.

For this reason, I like to conduct evening presentations for community members describing the skills that today's workforce needs, paying special attention to data based on actual jobs. The more you can back up your presentation with hard data, the more readily it will be accepted. Next, I like to hold assemblies for middle- and high-school students, in which I describe the changing landscape of work based on this research. I like to follow this with a workshop for educators, sharing with them the skills necessary for their students to learn, along with practical strategies for teaching these skills within the existing curriculum.

This last portion is critically important. Curriculum reform takes a long time to achieve, and many of the skills on our list can be developed using subject matter already mandated by the district—as long as the teachers are willing to incorporate project-based learning and foster independent lifelong learning among their students.

What About the "Yeah, Buts"?

Because some of the ideas you'll be sharing run counter to current perceptions, you should expect to be called on every piece of data you share. It is very important to answer all questions with cogent responses backed by hard references. For example, during a presentation for school administrators, one participant said, "Yes, but your job skill data were based on a national sample, and the needs of our community may be different." In this case I had anticipated the objection and had some skill inventory data for their community that I'd assembled the night before. This data matched the national sample quite closely. An even more effective response would be to suggest that the questioner create a skill inventory herself, using the same job-hunting Web sites mentioned in Chapter 6. The point here is that this information is not a secret, and is available to anyone who wants it. The quicker you can agree on the necessary skills, the quicker you can move to exploring ways to develop them at school.

If someone says, "Yes, but we are required to run our schools the way we do by state mandate," then you can share some strategies for addressing state requirements while changing the manner in which they are met. For example, it may well be that your state has mandated that every child learn state history in 4th grade, and may even recommend certain textbooks and other teacher-support materials. The fact is that teachers have incredible flexibility in deciding how exactly to teach a subject. Teacher-directed presentations that follow the "scope and sequence" can usually meet their goals, but so can more self-directed learning models involving student projects and student-crafted presentations.

Introducing new items to the curriculum is a trickier issue still than simply altering teaching methods. For example, in August 2001 I visited a school in Shanghai, China, that spends two hours a day on fine arts—music, dance, painting, and poetry—with large, uninterrupted blocks of time for students to express themselves creatively. Most schools in the United States seem to be struggling just to keep *any* fine arts in the curriculum, so achieving this level of transformation would probably take a long time.

Even subjects like mathematics are hard to change. Sometimes I think the only difference between the average math curriculum today and that of a few hundred years ago is that the textbooks are in English instead of Latin. We are in the early years of the 21st century, and yet there is virtually no 20th-century mathematics in our curriculum. It is astounding to realize that we teach 20th-century science, literature, and history, but that our math curriculum is based on material familiar to Euclid and Descartes. Some people don't see this as a problem because they feel that mathematics is somehow "complete" and doesn't need to be updated. One parent told me, "One plus one is still two, and always will be." I responded that breakthroughs in nonlinear systems theory have added the branches of chaos and complexity to our mathematical palette. If these newer branches were of interest only to theoreticians, then I'd be content to leave them for college; but the fact is they offer valuable insights into all kinds of nonmathematical topics, such as the existence of natural monopolies and many other issues relevant to the business world. To deny students an introduction to these branches of math is to deprive them of analytical tools they will need to thrive in a rapidly changing economy.

Addressing the Tyranny of Time

By this point you may at least grudgingly agree that changes are called for. Still, some may argue that we lack time in the school day to explore these topics adequately. On this we can all agree: the instructional day is filled with a host of activities and expectations that make it hard to explore new topics. One way to address this challenge is to see what existing requirements can be achieved in the course of exploring new content. For example, high-school students learn mathematical operations involving complex numbers. Instead of having students complete standard worksheets, teachers could introduce them to chaos theory using the Mandelbrot set—an incredibly beautiful and infinitely complex mathematical function created through the repeated multiplication of complex numbers. Because of the sheer volume of computations needed to create images based on these sets, computers are required. Students could either create their own programs to reinforce their understanding of complex number math, or use existing shareware programs to explore chaotic functions. (Similarly, in the realm of fine arts, students studying a historical event could create and perform a play or opera about the topic.)

There are many strategies on which teachers can brainstorm to find ways of fitting new ideas within the context of existing requirements. At the same time, however, we need to work hard to strip our curriculum of content that is no longer relevant. This is a long-term project, but is essential if true systemic reform is to be achieved.

Involving the Community

When returning to the cave, some will no doubt applaud your observations and dedication, but point out that staff development and student-support materials will break a budget already strapped to the limit. This is an additional incentive to obtain advance community support for your ideas: by getting the community involved, you may find a local cadre of volunteers willing and able to help out free of charge. In the past few years I've seen communities so galvanized around a fresh vision of education that a high school received a complete planetarium, a middle school received a complete observatory, and an elementary school received ergonomically designed chairs and custom-built computer desks for every room. Once the community knows that you're fighting for a successful future for its children, the coffers will often open wide.

Some Closing Thoughts

We are now living the future we worked so hard to create for our children. It may not have unfolded the way you thought it might—wild cards are played at every table—but there is no question that we live in a time of incredible excitement and promise.

Oliver Wendell Holmes once said that the human mind, once stretched, never returns to its original dimension. My goal has been to stretch your mind a bit by presenting solid evidence that the future will not be an extrapolation of our industrial past. In sharing these insights I have expressed opinions and shared data from numerous reliable sources. The resulting picture might not be recognizable in a few years, but the foundational ideas presented here will probably stand the test of time.

As you put this book down and go about your life, I hope some of the ideas I've presented will stay with you. I hope you share these ideas with others, and that in doing so, new communities of practice might develop to ensure that every student will leave school with the skills and habits of mind needed to thrive joyously in the coming years. It is in celebration of their bright future that I send you my very best wishes for all your endeavors.

REFERENCES

Barker, J. A. (1992). *Future edge: Discovering the new paradigms of success.* New York: William Morrow & Co.

Burmark, L. (2002). *Visual literacy: Learn to see, see to learn.* Alexandria, VA: Association for Supervision and Curriculum Development.

Cairncross, F. (1997). *The death of distance: How the communications revolution will change our lives.* Boston, MA: Harvard Business School Press.

CEO Forum. (2001). *School technology and readiness report.* Washington, DC: CEO Forum. Available: http://www.ceoforum.org/reports.cfm.

Christensen, C. M. (1997). *The innovators dilemma: When new technologies cause great firms to fail.* Boston, MA: Harvard Business School Press.

Gerstner, L. (1998, October). Keynote address at the Organization for Economic Cooperation and Development Ministerial Conference, Ottawa.

Gilder, G. (2000). *Telecosm: How infinite bandwidth will revolutionize our world.* New York: The Free Press.

Information Technology Association of America. (2001). *Bridging the gap: Information technology skills for a new millennium.* Arlington, VA: Information Technology Association of America. Available: http://www.itaa.org.

Laubacher, R., & Malone, T. (2001). *Retreat of the firm and the rise of guilds: The employment relationship in the age of virtual business.* Philadelphia, PA: CDI at Work. Available: http://www.cdiat-work.com.

Lemke, C. (2001). *21st century skills.* Naperville, IL: NCREL. Available: http://www.ncrel.org/engauge/skills/skills.htm.

Lottor, M. K. (2001). Internet growth zone summary reports. Available at: ftp://ftp.nw.com/pub/zone.

Machiavelli, N. (1998). *The Prince.* (W. K. Marriott trans.). Project Gutenberg e-text. Available: http://www.gutenberg.net.

Marber, P. (1998). *From third world to world class: The future of emerging markets in the global economy.* Cambridge, MA: Perseus Books.

Mars Millennium Project. (2000). *Mars Millennium Project* [Web site]. Available: http://www.mars2030.net.

Naisbitt, J. (1982). *Megatrends: Ten new directions transforming our lives.* New York: Warner Books.

Naisbitt, J., Naisbitt, N., & Philips, D. (1999). *High tech, high touch: Technology and our search for meaning.* New York: Broadway Books.

National Commission on Mathematics and Science Teaching for the 21st Century. (2000). *Before it's too late: A report to the nation.* Washington, DC: U.S. Department of Education. Available: http://www.ed.gov/americacounts/glenn.

NUA Internet Surveys. (2001). Available: http://www.nua.com/surveys.

Pew Internet & American Life Project. (2001). *Teenage life online: The rise of the instant-message generation and the Internet's impact on friendships and family relationships.* Washington, DC: Pew Internet & American Life Project. Available: http://www.pewinternet.org.

Plato. (1871/1998). *The Republic.* (B. Jowett trans.). Project Gutenberg e-text. Available: http://www.gutenberg.net. (Original work published 1871)

Reich, R. B. (1992). *The work of nations: Preparing ourselves for 21st-century capitalism.* New York: Vintage Books.

Sakaiya, T. (1991). *The knowledge-value revolution, or a history of the future.* New York: Kodansha America.

Taylor, F. W. (1911/1998). *The principles of scientific management.* Mineola, NY: Dover Publications. (Original work published 1911)

U.S. Census Bureau. (2000). *Statistical Abstract of the United States.* Washington, DC: U.S. Census Bureau.

Woodall, P. (Sept. 23, 2000). Untangling e-conomics. *The Economist,* 1–40.

WorldLingo.com. (2000, November). *The WorldLingo Quarterly E-mail Survey.* Available: www.worldlingo.com/resources/nov_email_survey.html.

INDEX

Numbers followed by *f* indicate topics found in figures.

technological fluency, 58,
62–65
technology
accompanying
Kondratieff waves,
11, 12
learning effective use
of, 63–64
Teenage Life Online (Pew
Internet and American
Life Project), 64–65
telecommuting, 42, 52, 103
telecopiers (fax
machines), 14–15
telecosm
expansion towards
periphery, 14, 16
explosion of, 12,
14–16
intersection with
microcosm, 16–18
Telecosm (Gilder), 12
telegraph, as wild card, 84
telematic age, business
location in, 78–81
telematics, 16–18
blending of con-
sumers' roles in, 18
effect on business-to-
business transac-
tions, 18
transforming work-
place, 76–77
telephone, as wild card, 84
telephone companies, 15,
22
telephone service, 15, 23
Tesla, Nikola, 88–89
testing, call for increases
in, 4
time
as abundant resource,
24–25
agrarian view of, 24,
25
overcoming restraints,
108–109
time-motion studies, 25
Toffler, Alvin, 24
trades, transforming,
87–89
transistors, 12–13, 83–84

as abundant resource,
26–28
future capabilities of,
28
reasons for prevalence
of, 27–28
as wild card, 84
trickle learning, 97
Twain, Mark, 38
20th-century curriculum,
107–108
typewriter keyboard,
layout of, 10

unemployment, 7
unions, 8
United Airlines, 76
United States. *See also*
United States govern-
ment
economy, challenges
to, 1–2
education presidents,
4
growing Internet use
in, 19
growth in information
technology sector,
19
skilled and unskilled
jobs in, 53
United States government
Census Bureau, 18
Department of
Commerce, 49
Department of
Education, 94
Immigration and
Naturalization
Service, 52, 102
UNIX-based operating
systems, 40

value, based more
knowledge than
materials, 30
VCR, as wild card, 84
VHS, 9
videoconferencing, 42–43
virtuous cycles, 9
Visual Literacy (Burmark),
65

web development and
administration, 51
Westinghouse, George, 26
Whitney, Eli, 31, 93
wild cards, 37–38, 83–84,
109
Windows, 9–10, 40
wireless systems, 14, 15–16
Woodall, Pam, 13
word processor, as topic
for instruction, 63
work
changing nature of, 5
effect of digital econo-
my on, 7–8
future shaped by
innovation and
standards, 10
in Industrial Age, 93
work contract, changing
nature of, 36–37
work distribution, 74–75
workers as means of
production, 31
workforce
change in types of
jobs, 7–8
as corporate liability,
34–35
expanding develop-
ment efforts for, 8
implications of broad-
band communica-
tion technology for,
30
preparation as func-
tion of school,
66–68
preparation needed,
2, 5
technology jobs added
to, 18
Work of Nations, The
(Reich), 32–33
work skills, 67
World Wide Web, 16–17,
63
WorldLingo.com, 70, 71

Yet2.com, 36

Zenith, 7

ABOUT THE AUTHOR

Dr. Thornburg has developed a series of workshops and presentations based on the concepts explored in this book and is available to work with schools, districts, communities, and conferences to explore ways of bringing these ideas into practice. He enjoys hearing from readers and can be reached by e-mail at tcpd2020@aol.com.